THE MIDLIFE CRISIS HANDBOOK

FINDING DIRECTION IN THE SECOND HALF OF LIFE

DR JULIE HANNAN

Morency Publishing

© Julie Hannan 2023. All rights reserved. No portion of this book may be reproduced, copied, distributed or adapted in any way, with the exception of certain activities permitted by applicable copyright laws, such as brief quotations in the context of a review or academic work. For permission to publish, distribute or otherwise reproduce this work, please contact the author at julie@drjuliehannan.com

ACKNOWLEDGEMENTS

To Freddie and Martha, thank you for your love and support, kids: you light up my life.

To Lucy, Sally, Cheryl P, Cheryl L and Emma – invaluable companions along the way, thank you.

To Richard, it took me a long time to find you. Your unwavering love, support, encouragement and patience made this book possible. I love you. Let's continue the adventure!

HOW TO USE THIS BOOK

IN PART 1 AND PART 2 of this book, I ask you to try out tasks and write down reflections, all of which are used to guide you through your midlife journey. You can also go to the resources page on my website – www.drjuliehannan.com – where you will find recommended websites and useful links which provide further information about midlife issues to support your well-being journey.

Case studies are fictional in detail, while still based on my experience as a psychologist working with midlife clients, and are used to enhance the reader's understanding and learning experience.

Readers can find definitions of psychological terms in the glossary and further references to external sources in the references. Both are at the end of the book.

CONTENTS

Introduction   *1*

PART ONE
HOW THE PAST IS STILL PRESENT   7

Chapter 1 – What is a midlife crisis and
how do I know I'm having one?   8
Chapter 2 – How did I get here?   32
Chapter 3 – What's the trigger   36
Chapter 4 – Why now? Where did it all go wrong?   41
Chapter 5 – What are my midlife options for finding happiness?   52

PART TWO
WORKING OUT WHAT YOU WANT FROM LIFE   57

Chapter 6 – The Impasse   58
Chapter 7 – Managing change-related anxiety   85
Chapter 8 – Liminality   103
Chapter 9 – Strategies to guide change   114

PART THREE
RECALIBRATING THE NEW YOU   129

Work	133
Finances	145
Play	149
Social	153
Parenting	159
Spirituality	166
Family	171
Health	181
Relationships	187
Sex and intimacy	205
Joy	211
Self-esteem	214
Comfort in life	217
Relaxation	220
Glossary	*223*
References	*227*

INTRODUCTION

You've reached midlife. A time of life when you may be facing many different issues or experiences relating to work (including redundancy), family (such as parenting, an empty nest, and caring responsibilities), relationship breakdown, money worries, and health (including hormonal changes). You're likely reading this because something isn't feeling quite right. It might be something niggling away at the back of your mind that's making you feel unhappy, or it might be something that feels so big and glaring, shaking you up with significant inner turmoil while at the same time making you feel stuck, overwhelmed, or pulled in many different directions from your very core. This isn't okay, this is no way to live. Yes, you are facing your midlife crisis.

And before we go any further, I think it's really important to say that for many of us, a midlife crisis is real: you haven't imagined it and you certainly won't be the only one experiencing it.

A PERSONAL EXPERIENCE OF MIDLIFE

My own experience of midlife crisis was a devastating time. I felt my life was not how it was supposed to be. I felt lost. Having gained my doctorate in counselling psychology in my 40s, I had a full client caseload and waiting list. So I set up my own private therapy clinic of psychologists, therapists and counsellors. Then suddenly, aged around 46, the career I had intended to see me through to retirement began to feel less appealing. I was making good money but really didn't enjoy managing other people and felt like I was attending to my clients' needs better than I was attending to my own.

I stopped taking on new clients to create some personal space to work out what was happening to me. But work had always been a big part of my identity, probably the largest part if I'm honest, so I found I was growing despondent in all this new free time I had created, I was unclear about how to fill it. I also began to wonder: was I lazy? Was I being a bit dramatic about my life? I felt a bit of a failure, but my clinic was thriving, so it made no logical sense. My kids were in their late teens, increasingly independent, and had their own lives to live. I had divorced eight years previously, had a good relationship with my ex, and had been in subsequent relationships. But I had decided to not date at this point to make time for myself, as I really enjoyed being single.

I started reading up on midlife but the resources I found were quite flippant and dismissive, promising me that midlife was such a great opportunity – but it certainly didn't feel like it. I turned to psychology books for more information and found some of the answers I was looking for, but without any practical steps to turn things around.

Overall, I experienced a profound loss around the sense of my professional self, coupled with the loss of my role as a mother (which I had not expected to hit so hard). My identity felt fragile, and I struggled to know which way to go.

So, with time and reflection, implementing everything I had learned about midlife, I rebuilt myself from the ground up, finding a new sense of identity and a new way to be. I used the process I described in this book to guide me towards creating a new life and identity for myself in the second half of my life.

In psychotherapy there is a saying that 'you always get the client you need' and this started happening to me. I started to get enquiries from other midlifers who felt they had lost their way. As I worked through my own identity crisis, experiencing just how fragile it is possible to feel during an unexpected life transition, I found I could easily empathise with these clients and take what I had learnt to help them find direction and who they were and wanted to be now in their midlife journey.

Bringing together all this learning and experience, this book draws on the clinical and personal work I completed during these years and shares all the tools and skills you will need to get you through your midlife crisis and out the other side, living a life that truly fits with the person you want to be now.

WHAT IS A 'MIDLIFE CRISIS'?

At midlife, many people can feel a sense of malaise, hopelessness, entrapment, dissatisfaction and disappointment. There may be a sense that, if you could just change the ONE thing that is holding you back, then all would be well. The trouble is you can't work out what the thing is. Even if you could put your finger on it, you're not really sure how it needs to change anyway.

Many midlifers can have a sense of:

- feeling lost
- life lacking meaning
- no passion or joy in life
- hardly recognising themselves
- 'is this all there is?'
- feeling like a failure
- being trapped and stuck
- feeling bored beyond belief
- feeling desperate to run away
- underachievement

- being totally unfulfilled
- 'how did I get here?'

Yet a midlife crisis is more than all of the above: it is a crisis related to our identity and about understanding ourselves at our very core. This book concentrates on this important aspect of midlife, that is, the crisis relating to our identity, while acknowledging that various other issues from midlife can be contributing factors to how we feel and how we are coping.

A midlife crisis is a psychologically challenging time when you are unsure about who you are or who you want to be, with an overriding feeling that the current you is no longer a good fit for the life you are living – it's not fit for purpose!

Research suggests that the idea of a midlife 'crisis' is becoming outdated because it overdramatises a time in life that can feel disconnected or tricky to navigate. However, I have found that many people do experience it as a crisis – an existential one, a crisis that threatens our very existence.

A midlife crisis is very much a transition of identity, as people struggle to answer, 'Who am I, now?' while also feeling they no longer connect to who they were. For some, it will be a traumatic process while others may sail gently through the transition. An identity crisis can affect anyone at any age. This can be very unsettling, but it seems to be particularly impactful for midlifers.

People find contentedness and emotional stability in midlife when their identity and integrity are based on an internal sense of self. This means they really connect with the person they are and feel they are living a meaningful life according to their own values and goals – a life they really resonate with. For this to happen there is an essential need for authenticity in what we do, how we live and our place in the world: to be who we really are. For those experiencing a midlife crisis, you may not initially know exactly how you want to live or what your authentic self looks like. All you might know is that there is a disconnect between who you are and who you want to be. The gap between these two identities leaves sufficient room for existential angst to creep in and acknowledge we are not being our true selves.

Transitioning successfully through midlife is not achieved by taking pills, though that might help some people with the anxiety or depression that might accompany a midlife crisis. Instead, you must live a meaningful life, and this often involves living the second half of your life differently from the first half. You have to work out how you want to live in the present and implement the changes required.

The good news is that you already have what you need to traverse this life transition and create a fulfilling new life for yourself. It doesn't require any extra money or large expenses because the midlife journey to a meaningful life worth living is an inward, not an outward one. Although a bigger car, a holiday home or an affair might create a bit of excitement or distraction and stave off a sense of under-achievement felt by many midlifers, big purchases and flings will only satisfy you for a short time.

What you need to make this meaningful change will come from within and means drawing on inner strengths and resources which you already have (for example, reflection, self-awareness, adjustment and action) – although you may need some support to harness and strengthen these resources to use them to their full potential.

DEAD WOOD

Dead wood can prevent a tree from growing and stop sunlight from warming the parts of a tree that need it to thrive and flourish. If you prune the dead parts of the tree, new wood can grow and develop. So it is in midlife, we often carry a lot of dead wood without realising it. Over time, it becomes burdensome, and redundant and can hold us back from moving forward. So cut it off and let the tree live again!

Dead wood in a midlife scenario can apply to people, friends, relationships, careers, old habits, obligations, rituals and regrets. These can be elements that no longer serve us but, like an old pair of trainers, they are reliable, comfortable and familiar but not necessarily supportive. To thrive in midlife, a thorough excavation and investigation of your life so far is necessary to determine the growth factors that you need to apply in the second half of life. This will enable you to be nourished, flourish and grow again.

THREE-PART DESIGN

This book is written in three parts to reflect my view of how to journey through a midlife crisis and how, through self-awareness and making conscious, informed, authentic choices, midlife can open the door to personal growth. It can be a transformational and reflective period in your life as you look to the future and finally fulfil desires and goals that you have knowingly or unknowingly held on to for some time.

Part 1 increases self-awareness of the factors contributing to your midlife crisis and enables you to understand the rules and familial self-limiting scripts that you still practise and that hold you back and drain your true self and energy.

Part 2 supports you as you put aside the scripts and rules that no longer serve you. Here you will pass through a new undefined liminal space that allows your identity to develop and change. In this space, you begin to recognise the essential life ingredients you require to live authentically and what meaning and purpose look like for you now.

Part 3 – emphasises reintegrating your life to include everything you have learnt and to practise living as the new you in your midlife world

So, let's start the journey together. It's time to revise, renew and recalibrate your life.

Part One

HOW THE PAST IS STILL PRESENT

CHAPTER 1

What is a midlife crisis and how do I know I'm having one?

CHAPTER 2

How did I get here?

CHAPTER 3

What's the trigger

CHAPTER 4

Why now? Where did it all go wrong?

CHAPTER 5

What are my midlife options for finding happiness?

1

WHAT IS A MIDLIFE CRISIS AND HOW DO I KNOW I'M HAVING ONE?

THE TERM 'MIDLIFE CRISIS' WAS first coined in 1965 by psychoanalyst Elliott Jaques.[1] It is a psychological crisis based around identity and can be triggered as a person becomes increasingly aware that they are getting older and that time is running out. Often this crisis is accompanied by feelings of having underachieved in life, being lost, bored and not knowing what to change. A midlife crisis typically occurs in people aged 40 to 60 years old, but can impact people a decade on either side of that range.[2]

Innovative science and medicine have doubled the human lifespan in less than a century. We are not necessarily psychologically and physiologically equipped for older age. We still have bodies and minds built for the physical and social situations of our ancestors up to 2.6 million years ago in the Stone Age – it's an evolutionary mismatch! We are inadequately prepared to adapt to the environment in which we now live. Stone Age people had a typical life expectancy of 20 to 25 years due to limited hygiene, illnesses, poor nutrition and the heavy burden of labour – hunting and gathering for survival was

Part 1: How the Past Is Still Present

hard work! In essence, we are not really meant to live this long.

If we fast forward a million years to the 15th century, the poet Dante Alighieri wrote about his midlife crisis in *The Divine Comedy* when he was 35 years old. This lifespan is more in keeping with the biblical expression 'three score years and ten', which suggested a typical human lifespan of 70 years. Since Dante's time, however, life expectancy has improved globally.

Nowadays, the average life expectancy at birth in 2022 in the United Kingdom is 83.28 years for females and 80.22 for males. In the United States it's 81.65 years for women and 76.14 years for men. And in Hong Kong – the best-performing country for life expectancy – it is 88.17 years for females and 82.38 for males.[3] These figures suggest that, at age 40, many people will have another 40+ years ahead of them to navigate! Due to increased life expectancy globally, midlife challenges may start to appear a little later in life than age 40 because of our extended lifespan.

Between the ages of 40 and 60, people become increasingly aware of the limitations of the second half of their life, whether that be physically, psychologically or existentially. They may develop a sense of time running out and of bodily decline, as well as mourning the loss of youthful adventures and creative ideas as it becomes increasingly challenging to hang on to their sense of self.

If any (or all) of the following statements resonate with you, you might be in the early or middle stages of a midlife crisis:

- I'm so bored
- I know I need a change, but I'm unsure how to change
- I feel stuck in my life
- My duties and responsibilities make me feel trapped
- I hardly recognise myself
- I know what I'd like to do but I can't motivate myself to do it
- I feel like I'm just killing time till retirement

- I want to feel passion and joy again
- I feel my relationship has passed its sell-by date
- I want something new in my life
- I feel like I'm at a crossroads in my life and unsure of which way to turn
- I need something different but don't want to upset anyone
- I feel angry and frustrated a lot of the time
- I need a change but the thought of it scares me
- I'm scared of making the wrong choices and making things worse
- I often think 'what's the point?'
- I'm selfish if I try and make time for myself instead of others
- I feel like I'm on automatic pilot a lot of the time
- I feel like I've lost my mojo
- I feel like my life lacks meaning
- I avoid people, situations and my feelings by drinking, eating or other addictions
- I feel guilty that I feel so unhappy when everything looks okay on the surface

Although many might attribute this feeling of malaise to depression, exhaustion or a busy time of life, the experience of a midlife crisis is fundamentally different to all of these things, as there is an underlying sense that something is out of kilter – somehow you have lost your way, ended up in a strange place and life just seems a bit pointless and unfulfilling. In addition, this seems to make no sense because, on paper, you may have achieved most of what you've strived for, and everything looks good. So how come you find it harder to motivate yourself, get out of bed and carry on doing the things you need to do? You can experience an overriding sense that this isn't where you 'should' be, it isn't where you belong and an underlying terror that whispers 'Is this all there is?'.

As a psychologist specialising in working with clients in midlife, I find that this fairly common crisis is the most underestimated, unrecognised and most ridiculed experience. It seems to evoke a less-than-empathic response from others – particularly our peers. Perhaps this is because many midlifers have the trappings of wealth, or the external signs of what many would define as 'success' and appear to be at the height of their accomplishments with financial security, the big house, nice car and a successful career. However, they aren't happy and that in itself is provocative to others; 'Poor old John, he's so rich and he's not happy – shame!' Or, 'poor old Susan, running that big company and spending every weekend by the coast in her holiday home – how awful it must be for her'.

The successful outward exterior of the midlifer who has achieved some material success makes it much easier to maintain the illusion that all is well. With wealth comes the ability to buy and spend money on new playthings to keep you busy and distracted from your feelings and in denial of meaninglessness in your life. Being rich can be a huge block to true emotional intimacy and to receiving compassion and understanding from others.

The midlife situation is difficult to understand because it's not necessarily logical. As with arachnophobia – most spiders can't hurt us so why are some people frightened of them? The midlife crisis is an emotional response to an existential issue – an emotional gap of unfulfillment, often triggered by a profound loss.

WHAT IS A PROFOUND LOSS?

On the whole, we tend to be able to process and bounce back from losses we experience in life; the death of a pet, losing a favoured object, not getting a promotion, the serious illness of a friend. We can process our grief and emotions in a 'normal' way according to cultural and societal expectations. We are impacted but it doesn't necessarily detract from our sense of who we are and how we feel about ourselves.

A profound loss is the loss of something you have heavily invested in, whether that be with love, money, time or energy. This might be a relationship, your family, your children, your work, your looks or your achievements. When you lose this thing or person you have invested in through a relationship breakdown, children leaving home, your job or career or life not working out as you expected or the bereavement of a loved person, for example, this can really shake your very foundations and can result in a feeling of being lost, feeling unsafe in the world, without purpose and can be often accompanied by a sense of our own mortality and that time is running out. This emotional chasm needs to be closed quickly – but how?

A FEELING THAT TIME IS OF THE ESSENCE

If you have a sense that time is running out, it can be really challenging to gather the enthusiasm to start something new or even to see something through till the end – we just don't have the time to spare.

Left unaddressed, a midlife crisis can be simply devastating, not only for the individual but for their career and family and friends. Slumping into a midlife malaise at a time when you might have a mortgage, work/family responsibilities, ageing parents, or be in the midst of a divorce, redundancy or bereavement, is the last thing you need.

You may question your relationship with your partner and become more aware of its superficiality or how only sex or social standing is holding it together. You may become aware of your desire for a more emotionally mature, fulfilling relationship either with your partner or a new partner, or you may decide that not being in a relationship is your preferred choice and that it's time to be alone.

In your professional life, you may seriously question whether your career is on track, feel you have underachieved, or have a nagging doubt that you're not in the right job and can't hold on till your pension kicks in. You may feel like you've made it to the top of the career ladder and it's all very underwhelming. You may feel burnt out and like you need to change your career to survive or reduce hours, even at this seemingly late stage. Maybe you've retired and life still isn't what you had expected it to be and the sense of malaise hasn't disappeared despite giving up work.

It may feel like you no longer fit into your life, or your life doesn't seem to fit you. Maybe your life is set up for a different version of you – an earlier, younger you – but certainly not who you currently are. It appears to be the lifestyle you chose, the friends you gravitated towards, the job you got excited about and interviewed for but now there is a mismatch – a sense that this life was chosen but does not suit: it's not quite right or good enough any more. The sense of fulfilment and pride you might have once gained from your life has disappeared or is fading and it's hard to work out how this happened. Did you change or did the world around you change? Either way, it is a bad fit and it feels disheartening. This is the life you were working towards, but now you're here it all seems a bit blah, dull, grey, samey and uninspiring.

When you find yourself dissatisfied at midlife it begs the question, where did it all go wrong? If you made all your life choices and ended up miserable then we need to really question the origin of those life choices. If you're seemingly doing the things you chose to do, then how come you have ended up so disenchanted?

IS IT A MIDLIFE CRISIS OR DEPRESSION?

You may not immediately recognise that you're having a midlife crisis because it can manifest in various ways and with different symptoms. Physiologically, some people might develop symptoms and notice a change first in their body such as a lack of energy and vitality.

Behaviourally, you may become snappy and frustrated with others and hear yourself sighing, frowning or swearing more, taking more sick days off work and avoiding or withdrawing from family or social events.

Psychological symptoms might take the form of becoming more emotional and being easily reduced to tears, insomnia, anxiety, impulsive decision-making or negative thoughts. Overall, there might be a sense of feeling trapped, weighed down by life, feeling a bit lost, a bit like a stranger in your own life – it no longer fits – and that life is lacking sparkle or meaning.

Cognitively, thoughts might take on a negative or catastrophic quality such as 'Is this it?' and 'There's no way out'.

A midlife crisis can feel like an internal conflict, accompanied by an age-related sense of underachievement, boredom, loss, feeling lost, mortality. This could be accompanied by some rash decision-making or out-of-character behaviour as you try to reset or shake up your life.

Depression, on the other hand, is less discerning about age and can strike at any time, again and again in a devastating way with symptoms such as a loss of interest and enjoyment in doing normal activities, trouble concentrating and thoughts of suicide. It may be caused by a wide range of issues from the past or present such as childhood events, trauma, having a baby, having a personal or family history of depression, seasonal affective disorder (SAD), substance misuse or stress. There can be some overlap between a midlife crisis and depression as both can involve symptoms such as hopelessness, low motivation, withdrawal behaviours and negative thoughts. Ultimately, a midlife crisis may lead to symptoms of depression that may need support to be addressed.

Part 1: How the Past Is Still Present

ARE HORMONES A CONTRIBUTORY FACTOR?

The purpose of this book is to guide you through the psychological journey of midlife, but it would be remiss not to mention midlife hormonal imbalances and losses and how they can impact enthusiasm, motivation and energy levels. This book assumes that you have had any physiological challenges investigated (e.g. heart, kidneys, bones) and that you are on appropriate medication and supplements that support you so that you can concentrate and focus on your psychological well-being.

If you haven't had the chance to do this, I would encourage you to explore this with your health professional. This will help ensure any health-related difficulties or symptoms are being managed effectively and not misunderstood as part of the psychological difficulties and the way they manifest in our bodies and minds.

Menopause

The loss of oestrogen, progesterone and testosterone for women, non-binary and transgender people can start in perimenopause, which can start 10 years before actual menopause (which has an average age of 51) and also early-onset menopause (which can strike at any age). There can be many psychological effects of menopause that cause difficulties: brain fog, anxiety, depression, cognitive functioning and low self-esteem. All of these can make the midlife transition even more challenging.

The focus of this book is to concentrate on the psychological effects of midlife and so I encourage you to ensure the physiological impact of hormonal deficiencies is being addressed. Many people will find these psychological effects reduced once their hormones are realigned. If hormones are realigned and you still experience identity issues, then you could then be experiencing a midlife crisis, especially if aspects of your life or becoming perimenopausal or menopausal impact you as a profound loss.

Andropause

Testosterone levels fall as men, non-binary and transgender people age. On average it is about 2 per cent a year from around 30 to 40 years old. In middle age, people might experience depression, erectile dysfunction and loss of interest, mood swings and irritability. It is wrong to assume that the reduction in testosterone is the main causal factor here because this drop is gradual and does not affect men in the same way as menopause and perimenopause affect women.

At midlife, people can experience a loss of interest in life and mood irritability. This is more commonly known as andropause, but these symptoms are nothing to do with a lack of hormones or testosterone. It is more likely to be lifestyle factors or psychological difficulties such as anxiety or depression alongside other factors such as a poor diet, lack of exercise, alcohol misuse, disrupted sleep and low self-esteem.

Hormonal Changes and Identity – Helen's story

Helen's sex life had always been important to her, and she and her husband had always enjoyed an active sex life. In perimenopause, however, her libido disappeared and she lost interest in sex. Helen experienced this as a profound loss. It really impacted the person she felt she was, and it distanced her emotionally from her husband. She felt depressed, invisible, fatigued, and hardly recognised herself as she struggled to stabilise her sense of self.

In therapy, Helen initially concentrated on her diet, exercise, and sleep, but then the main focus became her identity and how she saw herself. She attended a menopause clinic and decided to go on hormone replacement treatment (HRT). It took six months for her hormone levels to settle at a normal rate.

In the meantime, therapy sessions worked on developing Helen's self-esteem and firming up her fragile identity. Determined not to be invisible in society, she began to work on areas of her life that had always interested her. As a result, her mood improved. She felt she had something to say and was relevant. The social group she belonged to provided her with understanding, good fun and energy. After consideration about her values and priorities, Helen changed jobs to do something she had always been interested in and, although she took a pay cut, she felt connected to this new work and believed it was what she was born to do – in fact, she felt she should have done it years ago. Her husband joined us for a couple of therapy sessions so he could understand more about what was changing for Helen. As Helen began to develop herself as a person, a friend and in her career, she found that her sense of identity was more evenly shared across her whole life rather than focused solely on her sexual identity, though that was still important to her.

With HRT, and by developing her life, Helen found that her energy levels improved and although her sexual desire had returned, it was not at the levels she had known at a younger age.

Helen and her husband agreed that he would initiate sex more so she could become aroused, as this worked better for her. They also read books on and practised tantric sex so they could increase their intimacy but not necessarily with penetrative sex.

WHAT AREA OF YOUR LIFE SEEMS TO BE MISALIGNED AND IN NEED OF CHANGE?

Exercise 1: The personal balance wheel

- On the diagram below, rate on a scale of 1 to 10 how satisfied you feel within these 14 areas of your life. A score of 1 indicates very low satisfaction, with 10 being extremely satisfied.

- Once you have given a rating in each area, try to consider why your lower scores are so low, how you feel in each role, and why you might not find satisfaction within each role.

- Within the low-scoring roles, consider when you steered off course here and lost your way or yourself.

- You will need these scores for reference in Part 3 of this book.

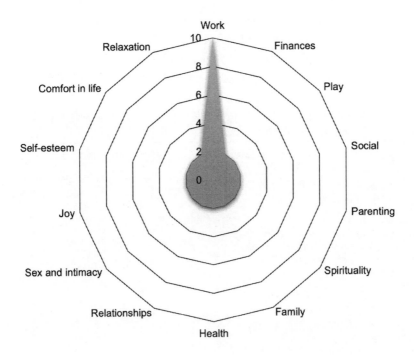

Scores

Work		Finances		Play	
Social		Parenting		Spirituality	
Family		Health		Relationships	
Sex and intimacy		Joy		Self-esteem	
Comfort in life		Relaxation			

There is substantial evidence that many people experience a decline in life satisfaction and happiness in midlife. The way this affects individuals can naturally differ, as it's a very personal experience. For many, and certainly for my clients, midlife does seem to be a time when people reassess their lives, achievements or underachievements, and whether they are where they thought they would be at this age and point in their lives. This can trigger a reappraisal of life for the person going through this, which can be disruptive for both them and the world around them.

Time, or the seeming lack of time, can be at the forefront of their minds and an increasing awareness of their own mortality begins creeping into their thought process. Annoyingly, this usually happens at 3 a.m. – the witching hour – a time when all roads lead to catastrophe! Altogether this time of life seems to raise questions such as 'How can I stay motivated when every day I am nearer death?' 'Do I have enough time (and energy) to make any changes I need to make?'

INDIVIDUATION

The feeling that these questions can evoke can lead to anxiety and feel like a personal crisis. To make sense of this with clients in therapy sessions, I use the philosophy of existentialism and Carl Jung's concept of individuation.[4] Jung was a psychoanalyst and psychiatrist from Switzerland who founded analytic psychology. Individuation refers to the process of forming a stable personality and Jung saw it as the focus for the individual in the second half of life.

A successful process of individuation allows an individual to live authentically and find their individual path. When a person individuates, through self-awareness and discovery, they develop a unique self-identity separate from any other person, separate from parents, authority figures and their rules and influences. In essence, they become their 'true self'. I think of it in terms of whom you were meant to be when you first entered this world, before you became moulded in the first half of life to fit in and became someone else. Individuation ignites your potential to become who you are truly capable of becoming and begins to clarify your meaning and purpose in the world.

In reality, individuation is never actually achieved once and for all, but is a goal and a lifelong process where you make decisions on a daily basis that support your true self. The challenge is to know what we need to change and how to go about this change. Alongside the acknowledgement that our true identity is misaligned, this process of change can cause further anxiety.

RESPONSIBILITY, DEATH, FREEDOM AND MEANINGLESSNESS

Existentialism concentrates on four main aspects or 'givens' of human existence that are intertwined with the meaning we attribute to our life. These 'givens' are responsibility, death, freedom and meaninglessness. All are significant within the midlife transition and, if not addressed, can cause individual worry and existential angst.

The extent to which we experience existential angst can ebb and flow in the lifecycle, but if you have a sense that you are not where you are meant to be in life, you may experience angst around this failure. That might be because you feel you don't have enough time to make changes, sufficient freedom in your life to enable the changes you need to make, responsibility to face yourself head-on to acknowledge that you got yourself here or meaninglessness that can give you an overriding sense that this life lacks importance, significance and value. Let me explain the impact of these givens a little further.

Responsibility

Without taking responsibility for your life choices that got you to this discontented place, you are powerless to be able to make ongoing, further choices as you are assigning your own power to another, possibly higher power. A lack of responsibility might sound like 'I was born unlucky', 'These are the cards I was dealt', 'Fate lead me here' or 'My parent was an alcoholic'. If you blame others for your current position, you risk putting yourself in a victim position.

Blaming parents for your unhappiness, misfortunes or underachievements when you are in your 40s or 50s doesn't really wash any more: you have to take responsibility for the choices you made as an adult. A parent's poor, unemotional or self-destructive behaviour can undoubtedly negatively impact your life, but in midlife, citing others' poor behaviour as a reason for failure no longer carries significant weight. If you are unhappy you have to decide to put that aside and assume responsibility for where you currently are in life in order to make changes. It can be painful to accept that you got yourself where you are today, by the choices you made. Once you accept responsibility, you assign power from external factors, such as an unsupportive partner or poor career choices, to internal capacity and then you can enact change and move forward.

Death

Death is waiting around the corner for us all, we never know when it is our turn to die. Accompanied by fear, these two concepts can really prevent us from moving forward in life. The challenge is how to stay motivated when, ultimately, we are one step nearer to death every day.

Anxiety about death seems not to be a constant threatening chatter in people's ears – we don't tend to walk around every day thinking 'Oh no, I'm going to die!'. In midlife, however, it can become more of a growing awareness of our human mortality, understanding that time is precious and we need to sort our stuff out quickly before we die.

Often in midlife, we have had experiences with death and dying. We may have lost a loved one to illness and this loss can increase our awareness of death and remind us of the fragility of life and our powerlessness within it. Many would argue that an awareness of death, without being overwhelmed by it, can be a great motivator in midlife. What better reason is there than knowing life is temporary to live a meaningful, purposeful life in this very moment?

Freedom

Freedom from an existential perspective cannot be separated from responsibility. We are free to choose and therefore must take responsibility for the choices we make and the attitudes we chose to hold. Yet how many times have you heard someone say 'I had no choice' when they are justifying an action or a decision they have made? Existentialists would argue that we all have the freedom to choose. As Stephen Covey said in his book *The 7 Habits of Highly Effective People*, 'In the space between stimulus (what happens) and how we respond, lies our freedom to choose'.[5]

In midlife, a sense of entrapment within your life will be a familiar feeling for many. You may notice yourself emotionally or economically tied to relationships that no longer serve you or property on which you still owe money, a job that pays the bills but no longer excites you, elderly relatives who need care and reduce your free time, and rising household expenditure and inflation that shrink your disposable income. As the great existentialist Jean-Paul Sartre said "Freedom permeates every aspect of the human condition."

Existential freedom is the inner ability to choose when your external choices are constrained. In *Man's Search for Meaning*, Victor

Frankl demonstrated this when he wrote of his struggle to survive in the Nazi concentration camps. Drawing from his experiences he said, 'Everything can be taken from a man but one thing, the last of the human freedoms – to choose one's attitude in any given set of circumstances, to choose one's own way.'[6] Frankl could not control the world around him and the chronic conditions he was subjected to, but he had the freedom to control his own thoughts and therefore the attitude he could adopt to the unavoidable suffering he saw all around him.

The freedom we have in midlife is that we can decide how we want to view our situation and use this as a motivating factor to change.

Meaninglessness

Existentialists often debate whether humans are meaning-seeking (we endeavour to discover meaning) or meaning-creating (we are able to create meaning in our lives). For me, both are true. I believe that having a life with meaning is not automatic, but that meaning must be sought out and we have the capability to do this. To lack meaning in life is one of the greatest existential terrors. What is meaningful to us can change as we age, so it is vital that our time (at work or socially) is spent engaged in meaningful activities and with people we value.

Overall, these four 'givens' need to be monitored to ensure life is attuned to your most current view. Taking responsibility and allowing yourself time to make important choices that are congruent with your true values, and do not leave you feeling restricted or curtailed are essential for well-being in midlife and will go a long way to stave off a crisis.

Identity threat – Jackie's story

Jackie came to therapy when her daughter Rosie went off to university. She had devoted herself to bringing up Rosie and making sure she was emotionally and physically available for her, unlike her own mother. Her identity was defined by being a mother, and now, as her only child was leaving for university, she became anxious at the thought of being 'childless'. She knew she had to let Rosie go and explore the world and had no intention of holding her back, despite feeling bereft at the thought of being without her. Jackie felt her whole sense of purpose in life had ended.

Being a parent had always given Jackie meaning in her life and she had no idea how to replace it. She experienced Rosie's departure as a profound loss, which shook her sense of self and made her question who she was.

She came to therapy to explore how she could replace what she had lost. Firstly, she had to process her loss and then tackle the loneliness she was experiencing. For Jackie it helped her to develop her friendships and reconnect with old friends.

Jackie continued to work but found her job had lost its appeal. Short days meant she had been able to be around after school for Rosie but now she felt she wanted to contribute to society more. She felt she had been a good mother, was a nurturing person, and wanted to help other people and give back to her community.

Jackie started evening classes to train as a counsellor and found she was able to truly empathise with struggling teenagers and young adults. She felt privileged to offer them support at such a delicate and formative stage in their lives. This work gave her purpose, fulfilment and meaning. After a few false starts in new jobs, she found a children's charity where she worked as an adolescent counsellor and supported many children into adulthood.

VALUES, NEEDS AND GOALS

Our values, needs and goals change during the course of our lives. To live well in midlife, our values, needs and goals must be current and related to who we are and who we aspire to be. Values and needs are closely linked.

Values

Values refer to what we find meaningful and important in life, guiding our sense of right and wrong and acting as the compass of life guiding our behaviour. Needs are a set of requirements you deem necessary for a healthy life and for your well-being.

Often, we don't tend to actively reassess our values and needs in adulthood and how they might have changed from childhood (except in therapy, perhaps). So, let's do just that:

Exercise 2: Recognising my values

This exercise clarifies the values in your life that give life meaning. Aligning your life with your values will give you a deeper understanding of what you consider most important and will help you consider if your life has become misaligned from your values somewhere along the way.

Look through the table below and select at least 10 values that really connect with you, to who you are and what matters to you as a person. (It's very normal that you might connect with lots of the values listed and that's okay, but for this exercise use your instinct and see if you can select 10 values that really stand out to you). Once you have selected your top 10, see if you can select your top six values that are most important and representative of you and what you stand for as a human being.

adventure	authenticity	autonomy
beauty	being liked	being of use
challenge	choice	clarity
collaboration	commitment	communication
compassion	competence	confidence
conscientiousness	consistency	contribution
creativity	culture	curiosity
dignity	discovery	efficacy
encouragement	equality	excitement
exploration	fairness	faith
feeling needed	forgiveness	freedom
fun	growth	honesty
humour	inclusion	integrity

Part 1: How the Past Is Still Present

interest	intimacy	joy
justice	kindness	knowledge
love	loyalty	meaning
mindfulness	order	passion
patience	pleasure	popularity
predictability	purpose	recognition
reflection	relaxation	reputation
respect	responsibility	security
self-awareness	self-care	self-control
self-expression	social justice	space
spirituality	spontaneity	stability
transparency	trustworthiness	understanding
wealth	wisdom	other

Write your six values here:

Once you have identified your six values, use the information from Exercise 1: The personal balance wheel (page 18), to see how present (or not) these six values are in the areas of your life you've identified as needing to change. Take some time to reflect on how you would be behaving in each of these areas from the balance wheel if you were acting in accordance with your values.

Needs

A need is something we deem to be an essential requirement in our life that contributes to our well-being. Needs are distinguishable from a 'want' – a want is nice to have – a 'need' is essential; we require it for survival.

Often, our needs continue to be dominated by the needs of the younger person we were. In midlife, you might find that the life you are living meets the needs of an earlier version of yourself but fails to address and satisfy the needs of the person you are now. This might lead to you being resentful of or struggling to do the things your life demands of you because your motivation, outlook or personal needs have changed.

What are my needs now?

What might your needs be now, and how might they have changed? In midlife, you may feel less need to fit into the world and your environment like the teenager you once were, but you may experience more of a pull to be who you truly are, a need for congruence or harmony in who you believe yourself to be and how you live your life and a real need to create a life that reflects your authentic self. In her bestselling book *The Top Five Regrets of the Dying: A Life Transformed by the Dearly Departing*,[7] Bronnie Ware says one of the main regrets people had, was that they wished they had had the courage to live a life true to themselves and not the life others expected of them.

A model that I use to explain midlife challenges and needs to clients is Maslow's hierarchy of needs: a human motivation model[8] (see figure below).

Maslow said at the bottom of the pyramid are our basic physiological needs such as food and shelter and, once these needs are covered, we move to satisfy the needs on the next tier of the triangle: our need for safety and security. Once achieved we can move on to fulfilling our more psychological and social needs, with love, intimacy and a sense of belonging being next on our agenda. After that, we prioritise our esteem needs such as self-worth and being respected by others. At the top of the triangle, we 'self-actualise' – we become all we can be. A midlife

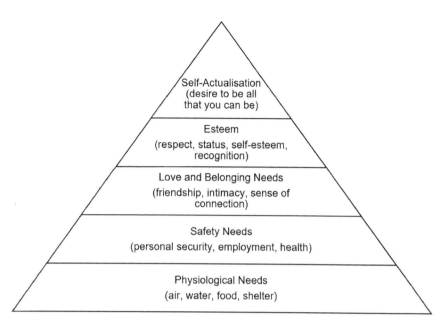

crisis can only really be embraced when the lower-level tiers have been fulfilled. In a war-torn country for example, there will be fewer people suffering from a midlife crisis as all energy will be channelled into ensuring that the lower-level tiers for survival and shelter are met.

You could argue that a midlife crisis is a first-world problem – but this attitude could unhelpfully belittle and trivialise the depth of angst of those experiencing a crisis. It could also feed the idea that we should be concentrating on problems of greater social significance and ethics – but try telling that to someone who feels lost in the world when their relationships and sense of solidity are crumbling.

Often, however, our needs are not so hierarchical. You can find yourself made redundant, unemployed, deep in depression and returning to the bottom two tiers of the pyramid covering basic survival needs. If a person's self-esteem needs are met yet their love and intimacy needs are not being met, they can find themselves moving down a tier, looking for a new partner or having an affair if they are unable to get those needs met within a relationship.

Changing values and needs – Jason and Sarah's story

Jason and Sarah had married in their mid-20s. They had similar values, having both come from poor backgrounds, and they prioritised financial security and safety as their primary values. Both career-orientated, they had forged a successful life together and decided not to have children.

Jason had dreams of continuing up the corporate career ladder and setting up his own firm, which he did in his mid-40s. Sarah was a successful headhunter and ran her own recruitment company. They were both independent souls within a relationship.

Over a two-year period, Sarah lost both her parents and found she wanted to spend less time at the office and more time with her husband, having holidays and adventures. The loss of her parents had helped her connect with the desire to live her life now and spend some of the money they had saved. Jason, however, wanted to continue working as he felt he still had much more to achieve and could spend his retirement having adventures. Their ideas were ten years adrift.

Sarah's needs had changed, and Jason's hadn't. This was a tricky time for them as throughout their married life, their values and needs had been on the same page. Now Sarah wanted something different. Sarah valued freedom over financial security, but Jason's values remained the same. They began to argue for the first time in their married life.

In therapy, they decided that their marriage was solid, and they were motivated to stay together. They eventually compromised, and Jason agreed to take one day off a week to spend with Sarah. Sarah went off on organised group holiday tours to fulfil her need for freedom and they agreed that over the next ten years until Jason retired, they would increase time together in regularly scheduled breaks.

Part 1: How the Past Is Still Present

CAREER PATHS AS A SOURCE OF CRISIS

Midlifers are often dissatisfied in their careers, and one quick way to try to feel better might be to change jobs. It is, however, essential to be fully aware of why a career is no longer fulfilling, rather than thinking it is just purely your boss, your colleague, the product/service or the company. A job is one of those areas you can change and still bring in income. However, if the fundamental reason for your unhappiness has not been addressed, it may reappear in your new role.

I often choose the Person-Environment fit (P-E fit) theory taken from the field of occupational stress to help clients understand why people might find that their career or life no longer suits them. This is especially true for midlifers who might hope that changing jobs will sort them out and all will be okay again.

The P-E fit theory[9, 10, 11] says that an imbalance between demands and opportunities in the working environment and the skills and expectations of the employee is the most important antecedent of the process of stress and deteriorating health.

In practice, this might involve a person wanting to take on more responsibility or get their creative juices flowing at work to enhance their personal growth, but the organisation micromanages its employees and opportunities for advancement are restricted. When there is a poor fit between a person and their working environment, their motivation, physical health, behaviour, and mental health can be adversely impacted.

We can apply this theory to the trials and tribulations of midlife. If you chose your career in your 20s, you might now need something different from your workplace. We spend such a large proportion of our day at work and if that work is unsatisfying then it will affect our well-being.

Consider what you need in a workplace and from a job. It might have changed from earning money, recognition and prestige when you were younger, to autonomy, helping others or flexible working conditions now you're in midlife. Then consider how adequately your current job meets these needs.

2

HOW DID I GET HERE?

PEOPLE WHO CAN'T FIND A deep sense of meaning in their life or feel unfulfilled will distract themselves with pleasure, so if you score low on satisfaction in certain areas on Exercise 1: The personal balance wheel (page 18), then you may find yourself practising some anaesthetising behaviours. These behaviours are a self-medicating way to block out unwanted feelings, and can include gambling, shopping, gaming, porn, thrill-seeking, drinking, drugs, sex, affairs, plastic surgery, overeating or scrolling on your phone.

The danger here is that we are wired to experience less excitement about the same experience over time. When something is fun or exciting, we get a boost of dopamine and norepinephrine to the brain – the happy stuff, triggered by sex, shopping, a new relationship, alcohol or other drugs. However, dopamine works in a cycle and begins to fade unless we pump it up again – we need to go bigger, better or riskier to create the same effect next time. And if we don't address the cause of our unhappiness, it can grow bigger, louder and require more drastic measures to quieten it down.

In society today, we are so busy 'doing' that often we don't think about 'being'. We live in a world of mind and body disconnect. In psychotherapy, we often say that the body is way ahead of the mind and the body will react to unhappiness and discontentment before the mind has had a chance to process it. The body might kick back with a reduction in energy, enthusiasm, vitality or libido before we have had a chance to process intellectually why we might be feeling deflated.

WHAT DID YOU TRY TO IGNORE?

Did you have a sense that your energy or libido, motivation, vitality or ability to love was compromised and changed? When did it take a bit more effort to be motivated, to make that extra business call, to get up in the morning or to say something nice to someone? When did your body know? Do you have a sense of the compromise that broke something within you and anaesthetising behaviours kicked in?

I often ask clients when did they start to try and dampen down feelings rather than address them? When did your drinking, eating, drug taking, staying out late begin? And perhaps more importantly, why did you choose not to address your rumblings of discontent with your family, partner, manager, friends or colleagues? Often, their answer will be 'Because I can't leave my marriage', 'Because I can't give up my career, I've got bills to pay', 'Because people should stay together through bad times' or 'Because there is nothing I can do about it anyway'.

The challenge with any anaesthetising behaviour is that we grow resistant to it. A sexual affair can hold your attention and keep you from thinking about the unsatisfactory things in your life for some time. However, as previously stated, with dopamine we need more and more hits to stay happy, the excitement can become the distraction and then maybe we'll need something different to get the same hit to block out the thing we are trying to distract ourselves from addressing. If the affair is purely sexual, and distracted you from the lack of intimacy and companionship in your primary relationship, then over time, as the affair becomes the norm, the longing for intimacy and companionship you craved before can return. In the same way, if you are bored with being in your job after many years because it doesn't challenge you any more and a new project distracts you from this after the new project is complete, you'll find yourself bored again as this hasn't been addressed, just shelved for the duration that the new project held your interest.

If your life lacks vitality and fun, you might buy a flash car to fill this void. Initially, you'll be excited pottering around in it but after a while, it becomes just a means of getting you to and from work or for dropping the kids off. You can't feel the same initial thrill at driving a new car forever – we are built to want more stimulation to distract ourselves if we are trying to avoid thinking about something else.

The car, the affair, the Botox, the new clothes, the drink – they are all temporary distractions. You might feel better (or great) temporarily, but the murky underbelly of discontent will rear its head again – that which you resist will persist. The real, fundamental issue causing you unhappiness in midlife remains untouched – you're just busying your mind. The inner work has not been touched: it is unaddressed and therefore remains.

Ultimately, if the underlying malaise and misfit of your life has not been addressed and recalibrated, the sense of underachievement will come flooding back and hit you in the face once the novelty of your new purchase or behaviour has worn off.

As Freud said, 'Unexpressed emotions will never die. They are buried alive and will come forth later in uglier ways'.[12]

Anything unaddressed or repressed such as unhappiness with your life will return and come full circle. Once the novelty has worn off, unhappiness will reappear until the source of the unhappiness has been dealt with.

You can make significant changes to your life without a massive overhaul that impacts everyone else, so you don't have to leave your partner, pack in your job, go travelling or buy a sports car – but you do need to cut off the dead wood and free yourself to live more authentically if you are to be happy in the second half of your life.

Unaddressed issues return – Alison's story

Alison had been married for 25 years and had gone through an acrimonious divorce. She and her husband never talked in order to address issues within their marriage, mainly because Alison wanted to avoid difficult conversations. During her marriage, she had begun to drink during the evenings to dampen down her unexpressed feelings of unhappiness and her inability to express her own needs. They had grown apart over time and eventually, her husband had an affair and ended their marriage.

Alison felt profoundly lonely and wanted to be in a relationship again but found when she got a few months into a relationship she would become unhappy and begin drinking again. This became a familiar pattern.

Alison put her dating on hold and came to therapy where she explored the unhappiness in her marriage, which she had been unable to express. Alison's core belief from childhood was that other people's needs should be prioritised over hers. Her father had been a violent alcoholic and her mother and siblings did everything they could to placate him. Enabling Alison to prioritise her own needs in life and not neglect her needs within a relationship was the main focus of the therapeutic work.

Alison worked hard to create a social life and joined several groups to explore what she enjoyed now as a single 55-year-old woman. These groups provided a safe environment and an opportunity for her to begin to express her needs and hear herself talk in an environment where she didn't feel judged.

Staying single did not address Alison's fundamental issue, which was neglecting her own needs within an intimate relationship and drinking to stave off feelings of unhappiness. As her confidence to express herself grew in her social group, Alison began dating again, determined not to avoid talking about her needs or neglect herself. This new expressive Alison did not appeal to all the men she dated, but over time she met a partner who respected her and was able to attend to the needs that she verbalised.

3

WHAT'S THE TRIGGER?

DIFFERING PATHS MAY PRESENT THEMSELVES in midlife, but it can be hard to decide which path to take without knowing if it will improve your well-being and not totally disrupt the status quo. Many people enter a midlife crisis or transition having experienced a profound loss. For some, the loss will be identifiable and very obvious such as a bereavement, relationship breakdown or a change in domestic circumstances. The devastation felt after these sorts of losses can be colossal and shake your very foundations – opening up questions about life, the universe and everything else. For others, the loss might be more subtle but no less impactful and can make people question, well, life in general! These subtle losses might include:

- loss of enthusiasm
- loss of interest in work, life, partner, socialising or self
- loss of status (at home or at work)
- loss of role (as a parent, lover, or partner)
- redundancy
- loss of youth, feeling older
- loss of looks

- loss of vitality
- loss of energy
- loss of libido
- loss of health

Any of these circumstances can produce feelings of remorse, anxiety, low mood, the desire to achieve or retain youthfulness, spend money, change your physical appearance, engage in a new romantic liaison, or make drastic changes to your current lifestyle.

Anything that you feel you have lost, that has contributed to your sense of self, identity, and how you define yourself, will have an impact on your beliefs around who you are.

A threat to identity is an existential crisis and can happen at any time during your life – particularly when you are faced with circumstances that challenge your sense of self. Perhaps you no longer see yourself as that person in a business suit, perhaps you haven't turned out to be the parent or partner/lover you expected to be, or your work as an engineer or a teacher no longer fits. Maybe being in a relationship is no longer for you and you long to be single. Perhaps a reduction in libido makes you feel older, less sexual and desirable, and a bit over the hill. I have worked with several beautiful women whose looks have begun to fade in their mid-fifties and they have felt the loss of being looked at and identified as one of the beautiful people and the flattering characteristics that have always accompanied them.

The same applies for company directors and managers who have entered retirement and feel a loss of power and position. Entering menopause for women and putting those fertile years behind them can trigger a crisis of self and identity. For some men naturally declining testosterone levels can lead to erectile dysfunction, which can plunge them into an identity crisis, becoming unsure who they are without this sexualised part of themselves and their ability to have sex. Many of my clients are going through a divorce, which is another event that can exacerbate a midlife crisis, as many people are left with feelings of depression and inadequacy and failure and rejection – even if you were the party who initiated the divorce. Having to redefine life goals that are no longer focused on retirement together can be disruptive and devastating and can leave the future feeling uncertain with a need to scramble around for a new direction, perspective and focus.

It seems that a clearly defined self-identity and sense of self can help steer people through the life course. To incorporate age-related changes to identity in midlife, while also maintaining a positive view of the self, stands people in good stead as they navigate this life period.

WHY IS THIS HAPPENING TO ME AND NOT MY PEERS?

Firstly, chances are it is happening to them too, but many people choose not to speak out about their struggles. We all develop and grow physically and emotionally at different rates, impacted by significant life events and experiences. You may be going through an identity crisis but seemingly none of your friends are. This does not mean there is anything wrong with you – it might just mean you are currently impacted more by life than they are, and you may just be going through a re-examination of your life before they are.

However, not everyone in midlife will have a crisis. A midlife crisis is an individual experience, based on many factors that can be potential triggers. Some may experience similar losses to you, but it won't cause a crisis. They might be more able to live with the impact of these losses and carry on but perhaps with a lower zest for life. Others will visit the doctor and use medication to enhance their mood or reduce their anxiety while sidestepping the real issue (that their life no longer seems to fit).

For some, life is 'good enough' and they can settle or tolerate the malaise. They may make a conscious decision not to look at the aspects of their life they are unhappy with, avoid change and settle for a life that is 'known' and satisfactory even if it's a little under par. That is their choice. Living an under-par life can be preferable to shaking things up, which can generate fear of the unknown. In a way, who can blame them for seeking more immediate surface-level relief? Let's face it, nobody really wants the hassle of dealing with a midlife crisis – it's painful, it's distracting, it can feel all-encompassing and can be disruptive.

Yet for many people who experience a midlife crisis, it isn't enough to settle for a below-par life. It isn't okay to settle for less than, to ignore the sense of malaise and unease permeating through day-to-day life.

You, however, are reading this book, which suggests that you are curious or acknowledge that something is amiss for you. This might mean that you are the sort of person who is unable to bury your head and hope that 'this too shall pass' because you tend to be active in your own recovery and, if heading for a downward spiral, you want to come out fighting.

Your life may have stopped being 'good enough'. The balance has tipped and the malaise you experience outweighs the possibility of ignoring how you feel and just staying as you are. It's a personal thing, a personality thing – it's your choice – though you might feel there is no choice but to act and change. This is still your choice – it means you choose not to settle for how life is currently. Life has to change.

This is the time when you may feel separate from others – your loss is yours and others who don't understand the magnitude of the feeling might flippantly offer you a solution: Botox, eat healthily, lose weight or a new job. However, you sense that this is no quick fix. You are different, and you know this is going to take quite a bit of sorting out. It's like waking up and finding the world a different place, and yet everyone seems to be carrying on doing their thing but, for you, that's no longer an option.

There is no quick pill to take to get over a crisis as it essentially means you have to do the psychological work to get out of this place, which can also be a lonely journey. This means examining your inner beliefs, your relationships, and your work and beginning to overhaul your life – even if you don't really want to!

4

WHY NOW?
WHERE DID IT ALL
GO WRONG?

Let's travel back to your beginning: your entry into the world, how you started to carve out your path in life, the choices you made as a young child, the choices made for you, the experiences you were subjected to, and your childhood powerlessness to change them.

Often, the first part of life (0–25 years) is spent finding our place in the world. In these early developmental years, we tend to set some life goals for ourselves, although we have limited experience of the world. We might have ideas of the kind of house we want, the money we'd like to earn, whether we want to be married or have children, the trips we'd like to take or the kind of car we'd like to drive. In the first half of life, we are trying to fit into the world – at school, perhaps at university, and in the workplace. We are trying to find 'our' people, 'our' tribe, those we gel with and, invariably, over time many of us do, at least for a while.

We decide at 16 or 18 how we will enter the workforce or higher education system. We decide which jobs to apply for, which interviews to attend and which courses to take. Perhaps we were helped to make our choices by discussions with teachers, parents, or friends, or watching family members who seemed successful. Maybe we were influenced by the media, or what looked cool, where our talents would be displayed and utilised best, or a desire for kudos, money, academic prowess, and so on.

Many of us will have had choices made for us: religious choices from our family of origin, and cultural ideas about which careers are suitable and which are not. Some of us will be living the ambitions and dreams of our parents who failed to make the grade themselves. Many of us will have just fallen into work and careers, choosing the first opportunity that presented itself.

As Jung said, 'The greatest tragedy of the family is the unlived lives of the parents'.[13]

People can follow these choices for many years, quite happily. We aim to fit in, not to be outsiders. I find it encouraging that people in their 20s and 30s come to therapy and address their unhappiness because they don't feel like they are fitting into the mould that society expects of them – not wanting to get on the career treadmill, not chasing money like their parents but wanting flexibility in their life and making the time for self-care.

This early acknowledgement of a misfit between their personal needs, wants, desires and ambitions and what society expects of them bodes well for younger people addressing identity issues early on in life, before it becomes intolerable. It shows that the quarterlife crisis is alive and kicking. I find myself envious and admiring their insight, awareness and desire for something better for themselves at such a young age and their reluctance to follow societal norms and expectations.

Perhaps you were the clever one, expected to be an academic rather than the artist you wanted to be, or perhaps you were considered a natural leader encouraged to go to business school and are now in a CEO position, just as the script said. You might hate this, because you actually loved dogs and wanted to be involved in animal welfare. Or maybe you were the one in the family who was good at maths, so you were encouraged to be an accountant when actually you were interested in people and wanted to work in public relations.

Undoubtedly, many of us would have expected that by the time we reached midlife, we would have our life sorted, be happy with ourselves and be comfortably off with a thriving pension pot all worked out. However, at midlife it seems that many people are still living their lives around these early decisions and lifestyle choices that they made or were made for them at a much younger age. In my experience of working with clients, one of the greatest triggers of a midlife crisis is the unhappiness generated from living life according to somebody else's life rules and choices. As Muhammad Ali said: 'The man who views the world at 50 the same as he did at 20 has wasted 30 years of his life'.[14]

Many midlifers are in the same career or spin-off careers from that initial choice, despite it being 20, 30 or 40 plus years since that choice was made. Have you ever stopped to question your choices and their origin? Let's consider other people from your childhood whose attributes you may have unconsciously taken on and not significantly questioned. In therapy we call them 'introjects'. Introjects are the unconscious adoption and internalisation of the thoughts, attitudes, values of others that you internalised and made part of your own self.

Exercise 3: What have I introjected?

Let's consider what you might have introjected from your parents. If you did not have a mother or father present in your life, then consider what you might have introjected from your primary caregiver or a significant adult such as a teacher. If that person who fulfilled that primary caregiver or significant adult role changed in your early life, then complete the questionnaire again with answers relating to the second or third primary caregiver (with separate answers if you are considering different people).

Question	Answer
How are you like your mother?	
How are you like your father?	
What could you do to make your mother happy?	
What could you do to make your father happy?	
How would you describe your father?	
How would you describe your mother?	
What do you wish your mother had done differently?	
What do you wish your father had done differently?	
When your mother compliments you, what does she say?	
When your father compliments you, what does he say?	

How are you like/unlike your mother?	
How are you like/unlike your father?	

This exercise will increase awareness of what scripts you might have been carrying with you from significant people in your life and what is considered good and bad behaviour and worthy of praise. Let's break this down into specifics.

HOW ARE YOU CHOOSING TO LIVE YOUR LIFE?

I always wince a bit when I hear clients say the word 'should'. On the surface, it is a seemingly innocent word, a word we often use and a word that can be terrifically important when trying to understand the origin of a midlife crisis. This is because the word 'should' implies a rule – a rule that 'should' have been followed. I see it in the therapy room with my clients. 'I should be happy, everything is going well.' 'I should be over that by now.' 'I should be higher up the corporate ladder than I am.' My response is, 'Says who?' 'Who says you should be higher up by now?' 'Whose voice is that?' This sort of questioning is the first stage in beginning to distinguish which aspects of your current life consist of the choices you made for yourself, and which aspects of your life are following 'rules' or expectations set by others – usually authority figures, parents, managers, teachers and so forth.

Family scripts are spoken or unspoken expectations and rules for individuals that may be unconsciously adhered to – that is you are not aware you are following them; they just form the route of your life. You don't necessarily remember anyone saying, dictating or spelling out these rules, they just *are*. We touched on these in the earlier exercise that may have revealed more about what you have introjected from your childhood and the life scripts according to which you might still be living.

WHAT IS SUCCESS?

What were your parents' ideas of success? Money, status, possessions, big house? What was their work ethic like? How did societal and cultural expectations and collective pressures back then affect their life choices? Did they value work over family time? Was money used as a status symbol? Did they keep fit or take regular holidays because they valued their well-being and actively attended to self-care?

Perhaps more significantly, what were their ideas of what success would look like for you? Who did they want you to be? What did they want you to do for a living? I wonder if these ideas form the basis of the personal and work life you currently follow when in reality your idea of success is different. Take some time to think about answers to these questions.

If you're currently in midlife you will be part of Generation X or a millennial, significantly different from the baby boomers (your parents' generation) and the upbringing they faced. The attributes of Generation X and millennials are resourcefulness, independence and valuing your own time and work/life balance, having choices, being technically savvy, valuing purpose and being adaptable to change. Baby boomers are known for having a strong work ethic, being competitive, having little time off and being disciplined with a regard for authority.

Perhaps success for you is more rooted in freedom, being flexible and having a social conscience. Is money as important to you as it was to the generation before you or are you less concerned about material possessions? You may still like nice things – many of us do – but are you prepared to pay the cost for them in the same way your parents did? Is it more about having time in your life for you, and the quality of the work you do rather than what you get paid?

Many people in midlife continue to replicate the familial, social and religious rules of their family of origin, which they have followed from childhood, often without questioning them. However, in midlife often following a societal script can be restrictive and outdated for the person you have become.

Part 1: How the Past Is Still Present

Whose dream are you living? Karen's story

Karen's idea of success was rooted in her parents' success. Coming from poor backgrounds and migrating to the UK in their early twenties, they had worked hard to give her all the home comforts and privileges they never had. Karen's script for life was to work hard, follow a known career path and make as much money as she could so she would be safe. There was little priority placed on self-care, but she carried an expectation that she should outperform her parents financially because of the great start in life she'd had compared to theirs, though this was never explicitly said.

Karen was a nurse, and her parents were immensely proud of her and her professional career, but the pay was mediocre. She was prone to burnout, always taking on extra shifts to earn more money, though she actually had enough to live on. She was unable to step back and recognise when she was giving too much of herself and needed to administer some self-care. She enjoyed being a nurse but the responsibility of patients and the demands of the job meant she neglected herself.

In therapy, Karen realised that her idea of success was not money-related. That was her parents' rule. For her, it was staying well, having a good work-life balance, taking care of herself and her patients, and having time for hobbies. She reduced her shifts, tightened her spending and moved to a smaller apartment. Then she began to pursue her interest in holistic medicine at night school. She was uncertain whether this would develop into a career but made that okay for herself by fighting off her internal critic who said she was being a bit self-indulgent and frivolous, and that her time would be better spent working towards a known outcome and being more financially motivated.

Karen managed to ignore the rules and quieten the voice of her internal critic by being aware that it belonged to her parents and not her. This self-awareness, coupled with knowing how her values were also different from her parents', was instrumental to her allowing herself to live the life she truly wanted. Though her parents didn't understand how she could give up a flourishing career, Karen was able to make the shift, knowing that if she didn't make this career change it would be a big regret in her life and she would be frustrated and unfulfilled.

Let's consider whose unsaid or unwritten rules form the basis of and shape your life and whether, on reflection and in full consciousness of the rules, you agree or disagree with them or aspects of them.

Exercise 4: What are the rules you follow?

This next exercise allows you to consider how your authority figures see the world and how their rules and 'shoulds' have rubbed off on you. This exercise asks the question: What are the rules surrounding these different areas of your life?

In the table below, the first column addresses typical areas of life where rules may show up. The second column asks you to write down and specifically name the rules that are lived by your family. Column three asks you to consider whether specific rules are part of your life. Finally, in column 4 I ask you to consider (maybe for the first time) whether you agree or disagree with these rules and to what extent. Most rules may never have been said out loud, yet they are often adhered to and assumed – we call these 'unspoken rules'.

Part 1: How the Past Is Still Present

Typical areas for rules	What are the specific/spoken or unspoken rules in your family?	Are you living this rule?	Do you agree or disagree with this rule?
Working (consider hours, and effort)			
Providing			
Friends			
Self-care			
Children			
Education			
Free time and hobbies			
Relaxation			
Being a parent			
Being a partner			
Being lazy			
Putting yourself first			
Commitments – can they change? What if you no longer enjoy them?			
Money – how much is enough? How much should you be earning?			

Now that you have identified some of the rules that shape the way you live, you have made them conscious just rather than a 'known' that remained unexpressed.

Take some time to reflect on whether you have been subscribing to these rules and for how long, and if, unlike Netflix, you ever stopped to consider whether this was a subscription you actually wanted. I also encourage you to reflect on just how much are they guiding and defining your life.

It can be important to discover whether you are living by rules and life scripts that are a misfit with your life and might begin to account for your unhappiness in midlife.

Exercise 5: How am I impacted by my rules?

Consider the following.

- Are you still trying to please someone else with your life goals or choices?
- Have you introjected someone else's values and rules unquestioningly?
- Do these values and rules even benefit you?
- How helpful is this rule you're following? How does it benefit you, if at all?
- Whose rule is it?
- How long has this rule been hanging around?

Now that you have begun to identify the family scripts and rules you may be living or how the authority figures in your life see the world and how their influence may have rubbed off on you, consider how the way you currently live your life is based around these rules and how you might live differently if you held these rules more flexibly, mixed them up a bit or deviated from them.

Are you still unquestionably accepting the values and roles handed down to you by your parents or other authority figures? Do these connect with you now in your midlife? Do they need to be revised, renewed, or redrafted? If you have a strong sense that your scripts and rules no longer serve you and that you need to revise these, is it any wonder that you may feel like your life no longer fits, and the rituals of life can feel outdated or that your career no longer suits you in midlife?

Think of all the ways in which people change from their teenage years to being in their 40s, 50s and 60s – perhaps from a shy, hormonal teenager who was new to intimacy and the job market, trying to piece together the jigsaw of adulthood, to midlife, when they will have grown psychologically, emotionally, and experientially. Why would your early life decisions resonate with you now? Is it any surprise that many aspects of your life might start to feel disconnected and not relevant any longer?

There will be plenty of opportunity in Part 2 to consider renewing these rules and life scripts. For now, it is about beginning to raise awareness of the areas which are most troublesome to you.

Exercise 6: New rules for a new life

To gently start the renewal process, just write brief answers to the questions below.

What is one new decision you'd like to make?	
What do you like most about yourself?	
When do you feel most alive?	
When do you feel proud of yourself?	
What was the best period in your life?	

5

WHAT ARE MY MIDLIFE OPTIONS FOR FINDING HAPPINESS?

GOALS, ASPIRATIONS AND CIRCUMSTANCES MAY have shifted over time without us actually noticing or saying them out loud. At midlife, you have the opportunity to realign yourself and your role in the world in the here and now, rather than repeat old, outdated patterns of behaviour and ambitions that no longer feel relevant because they were formed at a younger age and different stage of life.

The key to happiness in midlife and the second half of life is to live a life with meaning.

As I see it, you have three options:

1. RELIVING YOUR YOUTH

This is the option that many choose. This is the quintessential 'midlife crisis' that people talk about. Essentially it is a re-run of what has already been – just upgraded in some areas.

Those people who have affairs, buy fast cars and engage in thrill-seeking behaviour are reliving the first part of life again usually without fully addressing what it is about their current life which is making them fundamentally unhappy. They aren't fully aware of what the misfit is. So, they try to recapture something from their youth that they remember made them happy at that time, thinking it will reignite their current happiness because that's what's been missing all this time. It is a known path, they've been here before, many years ago, and it worked then, so why not do it again? They think they are doing it differently this time around – mainly because they are older. But the things that excited an adolescent do not necessarily excite a 50-year-old – or maybe they will temporarily provide a great distraction. This approach to happiness tends to be just a re-run because the awareness of why you made those choices back then, may not be completely clear, and so you unconsciously make them again and then wonder why you end up in the same place a few years down the line, once the distraction has passed. This is the easiest (not less painful!) option to implement – just do what you did all over again but with a better car or a younger partner. But the reality is, you can expect a short-term thrill that doesn't last and then find yourself back at the start again.

2. STAYING AS YOU ARE

There are two options within this choice. Firstly, try to ignore the unhappiness by drowning yourself in anaesthetising behaviour. Second, settle – don't dare to look or think outside of your current life. You decide to choose the 'known' over the 'unknown' and compromise on potential happiness and freedom, for safety. If you chose this way and you do it with awareness, not in a state of denial, then it can be a conscious choice that will make your life more tolerable.

Fear keeps many people in this stuck position. Again, if you consciously refuse to face the fear, it is still your choice and you have taken responsibility for that position, so there will be some degree of satisfaction, contentment and safety and relief.

Staying as you are – Rebecca's story

Rebecca had been married for 15 years. She and her husband lived in a big house, had a large circle of friends and had been successful with their business. They lived a very comfortable lifestyle with their three children in private school. Their friends consisted mainly of other school parents who were couples and had been together for a similar amount of time.

Rebecca loved her lifestyle but was no longer in love with her husband. Any intimacy between them had stopped many years earlier, and they were living more as friendly housemates. She knew if they divorced, her lifestyle would take a hit. She had come from a poor background and wasn't prepared to sacrifice the hard work she had put in, or to lose the house she had strived for. She also knew that friends would take sides in the divorce and would choose whether they remained friends with her or her husband. She was attached to her material goods and lifestyle.

Rebecca suspected her husband was having an affair. In therapy, she explored how she and her husband had not addressed the lack of intimacy in their relationship and how she was reluctant to tackle him about the affair as ultimately she didn't want to divorce and have to move home.

Rebecca's mental health was good and when she left therapy, she was comfortable in her decision to not rock the boat within her marriage because it worked for her at the present time. She was mindful enough to know that this situation might not always be the case and she might return to therapy again at a later date, if she felt unhappy about her choices.

3. LIMINALITY AND RECALIBRATION

True contentment and happiness in midlife can come from living the second half of life differently to the first, by making conscious choices. Conscious choices are made by people with full awareness of the motivation behind their choices.

As you release yourself from unwanted life scripts and rules that no longer serve you, you enter into liminality – the space where you begin to consider how you want to live your life now. You will learn how to take care of yourself in this transitional space and how to gently begin making significant change through self-awareness, conscious choices and supporting the self.

How you do this will be different for everybody. However, a good life that is connected to you and the present day, is authentic and satisfying can generate excitement and self-worth on a steady slow-release basis without the need for massive boosts and thrills because generally life is real, meaningful and good.

Part Two

WORKING OUT WHAT YOU WANT FROM LIFE

CHAPTER 6
The impasse

CHAPTER 7
Managing change-related anxiety

CHAPTER 8
Liminality

CHAPTER 9
Strategies to guide change

6

THE IMPASSE

Part 1 of this book aimed to help you understand how easily life can become outdated leading to a sense of living in a way which is disconnected from the person you want to be. It has also aimed to help your understanding of how experiencing a profound loss can shatter an identity in an instant leading to a sense of no longer knowing who you are. Hopefully, you have been able to identify the source of the rules and scripts you have been following and consider handing them back with a 'no thank you' to their rightful owner, person, culture, belief system, or social expectation. Perhaps you are beginning to understand why other people followed or believed them, how they became part of your formulated life script and how you internalised and adopted them. You will also be more aware of the 'keepers', that is, those aspects of your script or rules that resonate with you and that you would like to retain for the second half of your life. However, despite having some awareness of what's staying and what's going, you can still feel uncertain of your next move.

Part 2 of this midlife process will help you map out your onward path to further increase self-awareness and move forward, updating your life goals, scripts, hopes and dreams, ready for them to be actioned in Part 3.

It is human nature to find comfort in the familiar and you may be comfortable with old habits and behaviours despite the fact that they are no longer working for you. Although it can be tempting to cling to the 'known', change needs to happen because the current you is not fulfilling enough and not how you want to be and live in the world. The question is, how can you change for the better? In therapy terms, you are now in what we call an 'impasse'.

At this stage in the midlife process, many midlifers describe a feeling of being 'stuck'. There is truth in this, because, if we continue to do the things we've always done, there will be no growth or movement. On the flip side of this, how do we know which is the right move and how can we be confident of a positive outcome? The general rule here is that if you don't have clarity about the nature of your stuckness, then sit in the impasse until you do. Similarly, if you know the area of your life that needs changing but are unsure how to support yourself if you go on to make changes, then stay in the impasse until your self-support system is clearer.

Jung described an impasse as 'a disagreeable situation where you see no opening, no direct path'.[15] It is what Dante describes in the opening lines of the Inferno:

> 'Midway upon the journey of our life. I found myself within a forest dark,
> For the straightforward pathway had been lost'.[16]

I would describe it as a stationary, psychologically challenging space where you can feel entrapped because you have begun to recognise the aspects of your current life that no longer serve you and hold you back from being the person you want to be, and yet there is no obvious way forward yet.

When you're in an impasse you might experience feelings of low mood, frustration and hopelessness, which is understandable given the stuckness the impasse brings. To grow on a personal level, I would say that an impasse is essential, developmentally needed. An impasse encourages a new approach and triggers a process of internal conflict resolution – you are up against yourself. So, can you give yourself permission to let go of tired, unhelpful elements in your life and move forward with new ones?

We hold in mind that there is no guarantee of happiness on the other side of the impasse because we have never been there, and we don't know what it will feel like. Exploration of what is creating the stuckness is therefore essential before any new action is taken – I can't emphasise this last point enough! As I always say to clients: self-awareness gives you choices that make change possible. We need to know as much as possible about how making the right changes will support your updated life goals. This is what Part 2 helps you to do.

STAGES OF IMPASSE

There are three stages through an impasse:

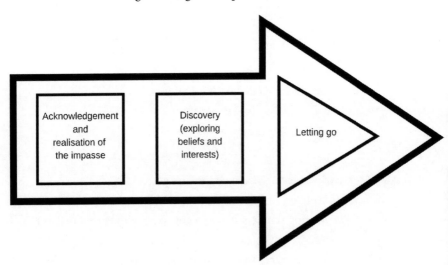

Stage 1: Acknowledging the impasse and realising you can no longer live how you have been living. It is too damaging to the self.

Stage 2: Understanding and discovering what's holding you back.

Stage 3: Letting go of what's holding you back and getting ready to move forward.

STAGE 1: ACKNOWLEDGEMENT

In order to traverse the impasse, it is essential to be consciously aware of the fact that you are in an impasse. Acknowledging, appreciating and naming your position in an impasse can prevent self-criticism such as 'I'm a poor decision maker' or 'I'm lazy and apathetic'. Give yourself a break! Life is tough enough without putting yourself through the wringer.

So, let's sit in the impasse in all its uncomfortable glory, and consider your life and the prospect of changing it. Choosing to pause and reflect is very different from feeling hopeless. It means you are in control. The journey through the impasse is not linear because it is based on your emotions and not a structured action plan to be followed. Where you are heading might not be crystal clear at the moment, but you cannot sit still for ever. Nor can you go back to your existing life as it does not bring sufficient happiness. We don't have a structured plan, here in the impasse, but we can ignite a process of movement and self-awareness.

Exercise 7: Explain your problem

Try and identify the main resistance you experience in bringing about change: is it related to a job, a person, your partner, your parents, your boss, an industry, money, skills or something else? Then consider what would be the result of doing nothing – what price would I have to pay?

Remember: You don't need to have any of the answers at this stage. This is about you acknowledging where you are. Trust in the process as you move through Part 2 and the answers should emerge.

Without thinking too much about it, take a pen and paper and write down (or record yourself on your phone), 50 words explaining your problem using this formula:

I feel stuck because _____

What I need to do is _____

If I don't change and get unstuck, the price I will pay is _____
_____

STAGE 2: UNDERSTANDING ATTACHMENTS

This stage is focused on discovering the areas and aspects of your life which are preventing you from moving forward and becoming the person you want to be. I'm going to call them 'attachments'.

What do I mean by attachments?

Buddhist psychology says attachment is the root cause of suffering and yet attachment is normal and, as human beings, we are built to attach to others. An effective attachment is based on trust, honesty, and security. Our ability to form attachments is influenced by how our parents or primary caregivers responded to us when we were young. Attachments provide people with a base from which to explore the world.

In psychology, we often talk about attachments related to people. In the context of the impasse, we are referring to attachments related to beliefs, people, and objects.

Good attachments can generate positive emotions. You might feel attached to your neighbourhood or your country and that can generate a sense of belonging and security. An emotional attachment to a loved one or friend can bring affection and a sense of connection. An attachment to an object such as a family heirloom can bring sentimentality and fond memories.

It is only when an attachment becomes obsessive, limiting, or all-consuming that it becomes problematic. So, at this stage of the impasse, we are considering only toxic emotional attachments. These contain a reluctance to let go of a belief, person, or object that has become unhealthy. This type of attachment no longer supports you, as it prevents you from transitioning to a new stage of life.

To let go of these toxic attachments is the only way through and out of the impasse and onto the next stage of the midlife transition. So, it is helpful to know to what or to whom you are attached, what that attachment provides for you, and whether it is limiting your potential and positively or negatively impacting your happiness.

Attachments to beliefs

Belief systems are formed at an early age (usually before 10 years old – identified as core beliefs) from experience and acquired knowledge. They help you make sense of your everyday reality by organising, understanding, and categorising events that take place in the world. They also help you to decide what is true or false and right or wrong. Religion is an example of a belief system. Because everyone's childhood experiences vary and children have varying needs and are raised differently in different countries throughout the world, belief systems between individuals differ. Our beliefs can guide and influence our thinking which can impact our behaviour.

Core beliefs are deeply held assumptions and judgements that we hold about ourselves, the world, and other people. Positive core beliefs can form the basis of our self-worth, but many beliefs can be very negative and the root cause of many of our problems because they limit our happiness, determine our expectations and how successful we may become, influence our thinking, shape our reality and affect our behaviour.

In midlife, people can begin to feel their belief system is limiting the quality of their life especially if they desire something that according to their belief system is not allowable or attainable for them. Very often midlifers have never challenged or updated their core beliefs which they set for themselves 30-40 years earlier.

It is helpful to:

1. Recognise your core beliefs
2. Understand their origin
3. Consider how a negative core belief holds you back

Recognising your core beliefs

The best way to recognise your own core beliefs is to try and notice themes in your thinking, especially if you think about things that will happen to you, others, or the world generally in an absolutist way. For example, 'Things never work out for me' or 'Other people always have better luck than me'.

It isn't always that easy to identify your core beliefs, so it might be helpful to think about a recent situation that makes you feel sad, frustrated or unhappy with your situation. You may notice that a negative core belief can be triggered by specific situations in your personal or work life or by general interactions with other people.

Another way to recognise them is to notice if you are experiencing a strong emotional reaction in life situations that feels too big or out of proportion to the event, as anything that can trigger our belief system can present itself in this way. When you notice this strong emotional reaction, you can ask yourself; Why am I feeling this way? What does this situation/experience make me think about?

Part 2: Working Out What You Want From Life

Common negative core belief examples about the self	Common negative core beliefs about others	Common negative core beliefs about the world
I am worthless	People will hurt me	The world is a dangerous place
I am inadequate	People aren't kind	The world is in ruins
I can't look after myself	People only want the best for themselves	The world is unfair
I am helpless	People aren't loyal	The world is uncaring
I'm not lovable	People don't change	The world is a brutal place
I'm trouble	People don't care about me	
I am vulnerable	People can't be trusted	
I am inferior	People can see I'm defective	
I'm not likeable	People are terrible	
My relationships won't last	Other people's needs are more important than mine	
I'm a burden to others		
I am unlovable		
I have no control		
I am flawed		
I don't matter		
I am too much for anyone		
I will never be happy		
I will never make enough money		
People like me are never…		
I am mad		
I am undeserving		
I am a failure		
I'll never be a success		
I am useless		
I don't belong		
I'm not good enough		
I am powerless		
I am unattractive		
I will die early		

How core beliefs can play out in real life

When belief systems are not updated or questioned, we can find ourselves living life according to beliefs formed much earlier in life, which can limit our happiness, personal growth and freedom.

For example:

Perhaps a core belief you have about yourself is that you are unlovable, because you felt unloved as a child and carried this belief into adulthood. Marrying someone can affirm that you are indeed capable of being loved, but the quality of that relationship might be poor. If that is the case and you stay for the affirmation rather than being able to provide this for yourself, this results in your happiness being compromised.

Maybe you have a core belief that you will never fit in and therefore you stay within a group or religious community because it is the only sense of belonging you have ever felt, but aspects of the group's belief system or behaviour push against your own values and belief system. You feel constantly anxious but you're afraid to leave in case you never find that sense of community and support again.

Do you believe you have deep-rooted mental health issues that you'll never resolve? Perhaps you never apply for a job promotion as you feel you might break mentally under the pressure and so limit your own success.

Perhaps you believe that others' needs should be prioritised above your own and so you stay in a relationship 'for the sake of the children' and compromise your sense of freedom.

Does your religion forbid you to divorce? As a consequence, you stay in an unhappy relationship, and your mental health is compromised.

Perhaps remaining in a harmful relationship has felt better than being alone, because you believe you wouldn't be able to cope without being in a relationship. The prospect of being single triggers feelings of abandonment, and so you stay but live in fear.

Clinging to a poor relationship like a life raft when it is past its sell-by date can be exhausting and draining but provides you with security in what you perceive is an unsafe world – so you feel safe but unfulfilled without challenging the core belief. But this can be a limiting belief and a dangerous strategy and one that potentially leaves you exposed to hurt.

Perhaps you have been treated badly in a relationship and attribute that other person's behaviour to you because of a negative core belief you have about yourself, e.g. 'I am worthless'. You are continuing to carry this belief into subsequent relationships and believe people cannot be trusted or will never treat you well.

Perhaps you have a limiting core belief that has been outside of your awareness. For example, you believe you will never be successful as success never happens to 'people like you'. As a result, you unconsciously sabotage new opportunities.

Perhaps you believe that a partner should provide you with all your emotional support, so you end relationships when this does not happen. You do not question the validity or reality of that belief and consider how a network of supportive friends might be an alternative way of getting needs met and remaining in a relationship.

A core belief that you are not enough – Daniel's story

Daniel was a serial dater but once he committed to a relationship, he always had an affair and never really hid the evidence, giving his partner a reason to finish with him.

Daniel's older brother had been the clever one who passed exams and went on to become a successful lawyer. Daniel struggled at school, yet he worked hard. Their mother was a narcissist and had always been very critical of Daniel because she felt Daniel's underperformance reflected badly on her.

Daniel developed a core belief that he was never good enough and that people would be always disappointed in him and leave him.

He sabotaged his relationships before his partners had a chance to leave him, which in turn reinforced his core belief.

He came to therapy to address this cycle. He began to recognise that his need to perform well, like his brother, was more about reacting to his mother and her chronic self-esteem issues, and less about his own performance. Evidence showed that he didn't, in fact, underperform, he just didn't do as well as his brother at school.

After consideration in therapy, Daniel decided he didn't want to cut ties with his mother. Armed with the knowledge that the source of his not feeling good enough came from his childhood and was fuelled by interactions with his mother, he distanced himself from her and kept his personal life private from her, so she had less material on which to judge him.

In therapy, we then concentrated on Daniel's beliefs about not being good enough and the impact this had on his romantic relationships. Daniel was a poor communicator in relationships and rather than express his anxieties about not feeling good enough and being abandoned, he shut them down and sought solace in another woman to make himself feel wanted.

Daniel had recently started seeing a woman and things were going well. Then his old worries came back to haunt him and so to not repeat the cycle, Daniel had to change his behaviour and communicate his worries with his partner. His partner was surprised to hear how he felt as she was very happy in the relationship. Her acknowledgement gave him reassurance and dismissed his need and quietened down his core belief. He realised he had been projecting bad thoughts about himself on to his partner. He began to communicate like this with her whenever he felt not good enough and was tempted to cheat. The communication stopped this deceitful behaviour.

Daniel understood that he couldn't always rely on someone else to affirm him and that he needed to take responsibility for building up his own self-esteem. Daniel gradually worked on all areas of his life that made him feel not good enough. He was able to affirm for himself that he was a worthwhile person and good enough to maintain a healthy relationship with a partner.

Exercise 8: Recognising core beliefs

Complete the statements below to confirm your core beliefs. Don't spend too long thinking about it, just see what comes to the front of your mind. If you get stuck, look at the list of core beliefs on page 65 and see if any resonate with you or help you to think about a belief that you do connect with.

I am _____.

Other people are _____.

The world is _____.

Exercise 9: The origin of your core beliefs

It's important to understand the origin of core beliefs. When you consider your statements above, consider:

1. When did you start thinking this way? When is the first time you remember thinking this about yourself?
2. Which experiences from your past contributed to the shaping and the power of these beliefs? Who else around you might hold similar opinions?
3. How might these beliefs be holding you back?

Attachments to people

Some attachments to people are healthy, such as those to loved ones who are supportive and encourage your personal growth. It can feel great to be around these people, you feel a good connection, you're comfortable in their company, and you can be yourself. Perhaps they're a good friend, and the two of you support each other, recognise and celebrate each other's achievements and spur each other on in the world. You might look forward to seeing them, have a good laugh and come away from seeing them feeling good and that all is well in the world. Can you think of anyone like that?

But there are other attachments that are negative and that restrict your personal growth and can become toxic, leaving you emotionally exposed when you rely on them too much to satisfy an emotional need. Often people consciously or unconsciously choose lifestyles, jobs, and partners that reinforce their negative core beliefs.

So, how do you recognise whether an attachment is healthy or unhealthy? The table below helps to clarify this in relation to attachments to people;

Signs of a healthy attachment to a person include:	Signs of an unhealthy attachment to a person include:
able to set and hold emotional boundaries	hostility
supportive	intimidation
good communication	co-dependency
consideration	stagnation
calmness in decision making	feeling unsupported
mutual respect	feeling misunderstood
trust	feeling attacked
enjoyment	feeling demeaned
energy and vitality	never-ending drama
feeling supported	often feeling anxiety
can speak up and feel heard	feeling drained
collaboration	hostile atmosphere
feeling of authenticity	feeling judged
feeling you can be the best version of yourself	unreliability
	feeling unworthy
	makes you feel unhappy
	brings out the worst in you
	visceral response when near this person (adrenaline rush, stomach tightening, feeling sick, loss of energy)

Attachment that restricts personal growth – Janine's story

Janine had been with her husband Dominic since they were 17. She was 42 when she came to therapy. She reported feeling frustrated and bored in her life and marriage.

Janine had left school at 16 and had gone to work at a local delicatessen as a cashier, where she met Dominic when he came in as a customer. They began to date, and she felt safe and looked after by him. He was a steady person; she found him a bit boring but reliable and loving. Janine had been sexually abused by her uncle who was staying temporarily in the family home when she was 11. He had threatened to hurt her if she told anyone, so she never did, until she met Dominic.

She felt the world was an unsafe place and no one could be trusted, but when Dominic came into her life, he began to change that core belief. She married him because he made her feel safe. By midlife, Janine's needs were changing as she began to crave new experiences. She had started to retrain as a bookkeeper and wanted Dominic to go dancing with her and try new restaurants as she felt scared venturing out into the world alone. Dominic felt threatened by the changes she was making and refused. He had no desire for change and was happy to stay in, but Janine felt she wanted more from life. Janine felt stuck and came to therapy to work through her feeling of being trapped.

To change her life, we had to tackle her core belief that the world was a dangerous place. This belief had begun to restrict her personal growth and enjoyment in life, by preventing her venturing out alone. She was terrified of being in the world on her own, but more terrified at living an unfulfilling life.

Processing the trauma of her abuse as a child took time. We had to separate that experience from her current life and recognise she was articulate and could ask for help, if she needed, from others. She gathered confidence from joining social groups including a solo traveller group that went away at weekends. She began to practise expressing and enforcing personal boundaries in her friendships, until she felt she could safely navigate the world alone.

Exercise 10: Recognising attachments to people

When you consider the people in the table below, do you have a sense that you are unhealthily attached to any of them?

You might find that you're often reluctant to interact with this person, don't look forward to seeing them, and feel that your energy is drained when you are around them.

boss	children/ stepchildren	community	congregation	customer(s)
employee(s)	famous person	friend(s)	housemate	lover
neighbour(s)	parent(s)	partner	peer(s)	relative(s)
work colleague(s)	spouse	strangers	team	union

If you have identified any of the above as potentially unhealthy attachments, see if you can answer the questions below:

I may be unhealthily attached to _____.

This is an unhealthy attachment because _____.

The price I pay for this attachment is (What does it cost me? How does it hold me back?) _____.

Attachments to objects

Unreliable parenting can lead to beliefs about the unreliability of others and encourage attachments to (non-human) objects as a compensatory behaviour.[17] This can lead to some people finding themselves attached to an object because of its permanency more so than a person.

Most people have meaningful personal possessions. Often sentimental objects are valued well over their commercial worth or replacement value. But it can be dangerous when an object such as a car or house keeps you trapped in an unhappy job or relationship because it makes you feel powerful or gives you credibility or status. The consequence of giving this thing up might trigger a grieving process. Another common object attachment is a mobile phone. Excessive use can negatively impact the quality of your interpersonal relationships, and your time with family and friends, reducing your social circle. Yet for some people, it can serve as a useful, positive form of connection with the outside world. To determine if an attachment is healthy or unhealthy, you need to weigh up the benefits of keeping the attached object against the psychological and personal cost of maintaining the relationship with the object.

Exercise 11: Recognising attachments to objects

To work out if you have an attachment to an object consider the items listed in the table below. Consider what an object(s) might be providing you with and how your attachment to it might be impacting other areas of your life. Consider how it might be limiting your personal growth and happiness. To help determine if your object attachment is unhealthy, reflect on how it might feel if someone permanently removed this object(s) from you.

alcohol	artwork	boat	books	car/motorbike
clothes/shoes	drawings	family heirloom or inheritance	food	furniture
gaming equipment	furniture	house	investments	jewellery
money	pension	phone	photos	porn or other addictions
qualifications	tablet or other digital devices	television	wedding ring	other objects

If you have identified any of the above as potentially unhealthy attachments, see if you can answer the questions below:

I may be unhealthily attached to _____.

This is an unhealthy attachment because _____.

The price I pay for this attachment is (What does it cost me? How does it hold me back?)_____.

Part 2: Working Out What You Want From Life

Object attachment – Steve's story

Steve felt uncomfortable in groups. He was self-employed and worked as a website designer. He spent a great deal of his working day on his own responding to emails and texts and an increasing amount of his free time on social media or playing games for entertainment rather than interacting with real people. Steve felt increasingly isolated and lonely. He wanted a relationship, but his attachment to his phone and his gaming took up his time and helped him to avoid his fear, which was interacting with others.

He came to therapy as his mother had commented that he never went out and he would not find a partner if he never socialised.

He agreed to try attending a social group with less emphasis on finding a partner and more on being in the regular company of others. He joined a dog-walking group with his bulldog, Myla, where the dogs' exercise was the main priority. Friendship was important but not the focus of the group, so he found he could engage with other people in a more relaxed manner. Often the group would pop into a pub for a quick drink after a five-mile walk, which he really enjoyed.

Gaining confidence, he then joined a local hockey team where sport and winning matches were the priorities, with fewer one-to-one interactions with people. There were hockey club socials and mixed hockey tournaments with the ladies' team which put him in the company of others in a non-pressurised way.

Steve reduced screen time on his phone because he had created a life for himself and made friends. He became less concerned about starting a relationship as he had created a social life and felt that in time, he would meet someone now that he had positioned his life to make this happen.

STAGE 3: LETTING GO

I'm not going to pretend that this is going to be easy. It really isn't. Some people spend their lives tied into emotional bonds and attachments. This is a tricky stage but managing it could set you up differently for the rest of your life and move you on to the next stage of the midlife journey: liminality.

We need to break the bond of unhelpful attachments, so they don't continue to dominate our lives and keep us stuck. We must be able to move towards feeling more authentic and leading happier more fulfilling lives. When you become unattached, you are back in control and in the driving seat of your own life.

The first essential skill you need to learn is how to unattach or change an existing attachment in a way that now positively works for you. I will cover this below, followed by some additional skills: managing your anxiety, negative thought processes and boosting self-compassion, which will be covered in the next three chapters.

So, by now you have recognised the need to let go of unhealthy attachments in order to move forwards. But letting go doesn't necessarily mean giving up!

There are three options here:

1. Keep the attachment and change your attitude/behaviour/interactions toward it so that it becomes emotionally healthier and supports your personal growth.

2. Replace the attachment so your needs continue to be met, but from a healthier source.

3. Go it alone, discard the attachment and learn new ways to manage your emotions yourself.

Whichever option you choose, you need to be clear about the answers to the following questions to boost and maintain your motivation to continue

- If I could let go of this core belief/person/object how would my life change for the better?
- What is the personal cost I pay if I keep this negative core belief/person/object in my life?
- What is my immediate need that it is essential I meet when this attachment ends? How could I get this support differently and what would I need for this to happen? (This might involve new skills, a wider social network, money, a safe place, emotional support, new living arrangements, legal advice, therapy – be as specific as you can.)

Now to the nitty gritty...

HOW TO UNATTACH FROM A SELF-LIMITING CORE BELIEF

These negative self-perceptions can be so damaging to your growth and happiness in the world. They are impossible to change when they are unconsciously held beliefs, but the previous exercises will have helped make the unconscious beliefs conscious. It's only when they become conscious that you can begin to tackle and challenge them.

The way to change a self-limiting belief system is to recognise its role in your life and its origin. Working through the following steps can be helpful.

1. Question the universality of the belief. Does it apply to everyone? If it doesn't why does it apply particularly to you? (For example, do you think 'I am worthless, therefore everyone is worthless'?)
2. Question the validity of the belief. Is there any evidence in your life where this belief has not been upheld?

3. Test the validity of the belief. If you said this belief about yourself to a trusted colleague or friend, would they agree?

4. Identify the origin of the limiting belief. Was this based on a passing comment when you were younger? Was this more about somebody else's issue which you have taken onboard as your own?

5. Dare to consider what if this belief was not true. How would your life change? If you hold a limiting belief such as 'I'm not clever', or 'I am powerless', consider what your world could look like if it turned out that you are clever or have power. What possibilities now present themselves? What could you become, what might you now achieve? Use these thoughts and possibilities as a way of finding out what you might truly desire for yourself and as a motivator for change.

6. If the belief is true, i.e. you are lacking something fundamental that you rely on others to provide for you, then this needs addressing. Clarify the additional skills, support, or knowledge you could be missing. What new behaviour is required and what support will you need to create change? I often tell clients that they don't need to learn anything new: the skills they are applying at home or in the workplace are transferable. So, for example, if they can give a concise presentation to a group of people in the workplace, they would be able to write accurately to a partner about what is happening for them. They have the articulation skills but may need to do some inner work and be clear about the purpose and direction of the conversation.

7. Take responsibility for your limiting core beliefs. Waiting for the world or someone else to provide you with evidence to disprove your negative core belief can be a long wait. It also assigns the power to change to others, to what psychologists

call an 'external locus of control'. However, when you take responsibility for change you assign power into your own capable hands – an 'internal locus of control'. You can then start to effect change rather than passively waiting for things to happen to you. Your behaviour then shapes your life and changes your identity.

8. Recognise the triggers that make these beliefs loud in your head. Is it something someone has said or is it something you saw someone do? For example, if a couple of your friends bumped into each other and stopped for a coffee, would it trigger a belief which tells you no one likes you or that people don't care about you?

9. Change behaviour – take a calculated risk and confront your belief, however small, to see If you can produce a different result. For example, if you think you are unlovable, ask someone you are close with if they love you. Study and sit an exam to overcome a core belief that you are stupid. Ask a friend if they think you are worthless.

10. If you find it too hard to challenge your beliefs, consider seeing a therapist to help you gain a different perspective. For further support, stay around people who can positively support you in this new way of thinking and who are rooting for your success. Cognitive behavioural therapy, which will be discussed further in Chapter 7, can help you distinguish between different types of unhelpful thoughts and negative thinking patterns and help you change them.

HOW TO UNATTACH FROM AN UNHEALTHY RELATIONSHIP OR PERSON

Working through the following steps can be helpful.

1. Recognise the role this person plays in your life and clarify what the attachment provides you with. Does the relationship validate you in some way that you believe isn't possible on your own? Be clear about how it has become unhealthy and how it hinders your happiness in life.

2. Keep in mind that to unattach from an unhealthy relationship can take time and may happen in stages. There is no need to cut things off immediately and leave yourself susceptible to emotional neglect and returning to the relationship. You may also be able to find a way to change the unhealthy attachment without leaving the relationship e.g. by creating different dynamics, talking with each other and learning how to communicate effectively. You could both take responsibility for your part in the relationship and begin to change problematic behaviours.

3. Open up communication. You can speak with the person and see if you both acknowledge there are problems within the relationship. Be clear about how you would like things to change before you begin the conversation. To effect change, both parties must be motivated to do so. Often one party (most likely you in this scenario) will be more motivated to change than the other. Set agreements and negotiate and see if you can continue with the relationship but still thrive and move forward.

4. If negotiation and communication is a non-starter, finishing a relationship and walking away and staying away will be more challenging if you don't have alternative support avail-

able to you. Consider how you can access support from a healthier source when the attachment ends.

5. Increase social connections and create more independence by cultivating a more holistic fulfilling life. What social support can you utilise to support you emotionally as you make changes? Begin to start a social network of like-minded people with like-minded interests. Many ideas to support this time of life are available in Part 3 of this book.

6. You'll need to focus on your self-care as you unattach. Eat well, sleep well and exercise. Managing the way you speak to yourself compassionately will be covered in the next chapter.

7. Keep motivated by being clear about the potential benefits of letting go of this attachment to keep you on track as you begin to make changes.

8. Differentiate between the attachment and the environment. Is it the relationship that is unhealthy, while the environment is supportive? For example, you can have an unhealthy attachment to your work, putting in too many hours, obsessing over it and defining yourself only by your job, yet your co-workers and boss are all decent people who often encourage you to go home, take care of yourself and not work overtime. Alternatively, if your workload is relentless, the company has poor management communication, the leadership is poor and your co-workers are unmotivated while you are enthusiastic and want to progress, then perhaps it's time to start looking to work for a new organisation with a different working environment and culture.

9. Determine where you are going. If you are leaving a bad work environment then run towards something, not just away from something, especially if you need to continue earning.

Be clear about what aspects of the working environment did not suit your values so you can align your next working environment to support those values.

Supportive ideas for making changes can be found in Part 3

HOW TO UNATTACH FROM AN OBJECT

Happiness is not dependent on how many things or possessions you have, but a nourished inner life. Again, it isn't necessary to rid yourself of all your possessions – we all like to have a few nice things around because they can be pleasing to use or look at. You just have to be careful that you're not reliant on possessions to fill an emotional gap.

We buy objects because we believe they will make us happier in life. Look around, and see what else could fill this gap. Working through the following steps can be helpful.

1. Understanding and be clear about why this object keeps you attached. What does it have that you need? It's a risk when you attribute values and needs to your possessions and money, so it's important to recognise what this object supplies for you.

2. Appreciate what the benefits might be if you undo your attachment to this object.

3. Identify the source of the emotional trigger that makes you turn to this object for reassurance. For example, if you are feeling lonely, do you turn to your phone for connection with the outside world? Yet, this keeps you away from the outside world. Joining a social group would/might be more advantageous for you and potentially enable you to make real friends.

4. Tackle the underlying emotion. If you have a core belief that you are inferior, do you have to own a big expensive object like a house or car to feel good about yourself and equal? What's the price you pay? Perhaps you are trapped paying an enormous mortgage working in a job you hate to own a house that boosts your sense of self. If you overcame your feelings of inferiority through inner work or self-compassion, you could free yourself financially from an object which is expensive to maintain.

5. Mindfully engage with your object. Reduce time spent with the object by scheduling time to use it (for example allow one hour a day with it, or four 15-minute bursts of time, then reducing that time over a month). Alternatively, physically separate yourself from the object. Find alternative ways to manage the emotions you feel. If food is your distraction from working through challenging emotions, then don't have junk food in the house. If your phone stops you from interacting with real people, then leave it to charge up in another room at night so you are not able to reach for it in the small hours.

6. Reduce contact with the object. You will need to find other ways to manage the emotion that this will trigger. Change the behaviour, socialise, take a hot bath, relax or walk, until that emotion resolves. Or contact a friend who can support you.

7. Work on your relationships. Change your social life. Great life satisfaction can be had by helping others and having new experiences.

8. Seek out professional help and work on the underlying emotions and new behavioural strategies which is manifesting itself in your compensatory behaviour.

Supportive ideas for making changes can be found in Part 3. Whichever you chose you will need to manage your emotions, thoughts (cognitions) and behavioural responses to change. The next chapter will guide you, helping you to release yourself from the weight of compromised attachment, and reach liminality, that space where you can start your transition to a more positive midlife.

7

MANAGING CHANGE-RELATED ANXIETY

THE ORIGINAL MEANING OF THE psychological term xenophobia is fear of the unknown. We are not built to tolerate uncertainty – it makes us anxious! Uncharted territory can be a nerve-racking business. At this stage, we don't know how we will experience letting go or changing existing unhealthy attachments, or if we will be able to find alternative resources from within or from others. We don't know how long it will take us to form an authentic identity that fits. All this causes us anxiety. We are only human, after all, and we don't like being stuck in situations that we might struggle to get out of, especially ones we find stressful. For some people, this can trigger our flight/flight response – especially given that we don't know what awaits us on the other side of the impasse. We don't know how long it will be until we reach this unknown place.

It is essential that you pause in this next phase. Don't make quick decisions or take action to alleviate the discomfort of letting go of attachments, as sudden impulsive actions might mainly focus on alleviating anxiety and are not necessarily good for psychological progress. In fact, they can push you deeper into the stuckness.

This is the mistake many people make in midlife – they make impulsive decisions which ultimately don't really work for them long term. Some people may change jobs to relieve anxiety, when the reality is that they outgrew that career and any interest in that work many years previously. Some people have an affair to revitalise themselves and drum up some excitement. They think they are moving forward when they're not actually addressing underlying issues within their primary relationship. They are not reflecting on their contribution to issues or learning from them. Others will move house, taking all their existing worries and issues with them to a new set of walls.

These are short-term, panic-induced moves and, once the novelty of the new job, partner or home has worn off, the underlying malaise and challenges from before (such as unhappiness, loneliness, boredom, or poor relationship) will return. They will be back in the impasse. So, we must learn to manage the anxiety of having cut off old attachments while not yet knowing who we are or who we will become. Techniques are needed to calm our responses to threat, so that we can make changes, sit still in a new space, and wait until the road ahead becomes a little clearer. Then we can make our next move.

UNDERSTANDING OUR HUMAN RESPONSE TO THREAT

As a first step in learning to manage anxiety, it can help to understand how our mind and body work when we feel anxious or under threat.

In therapy, much of my work with clients can focus on removing threats from their lives, increasing their ability to cope and fostering a sense of agency and autonomy – actual or perceived – in order to reduce physiological symptoms of anxiety and fear.

There is a difference between anxiety and fear. Fear is a protective response to an identifiable threat, such as being attacked. We have a strong physiological reaction, which is our autonomic arousal kicking in, and we experience a fight/flight/freeze response where we either submit, fight or flee the scene. Our anxiety response is physiologically similar to our fear response: we experience increased autonomic arousal but there is no identifiable threat. We are anxious at the prospect of a potential threat that may or may not happen (i.e. the possibility of being attacked).

Key models of anxiety-related psychopathology describe anxiety as having three key components.

1. The physiological component is how our autonomic nervous system responds when activated and shows up in our physical/bodily symptoms.

2. Our cognitive response (the way we think about our situation) is how we interpret what is happening around us, how our body is feeling (environmental and physiological stimuli).

3. Our behavioural response, which is how we react to the stimuli (cognitive, environmental and physiological).

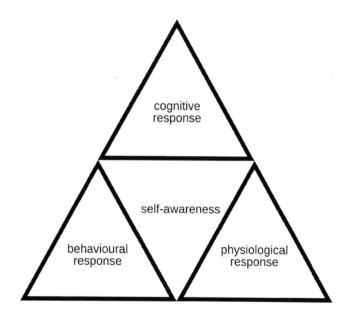

You will need to manage all three areas using self-awareness as your guide, as this is central to well-being and tolerating uncertainty. Being aware of how we are impacted in these three ways enables us to make choices to manage ourselves and our reactions better in a more controlled way.

UNDERSTANDING AND MANAGING YOUR PHYSIOLOGICAL RESPONSE TO THREAT

Our bodies have an autonomic nervous system (ANS), which is the central component of emotion and motivated action. The ANS consists of a sympathetic nervous system (SNS) and a parasympathetic nervous system (PNS).

Your SNS takes responsibility for many functions within the body that need no conscious control because they happen automatically, such as heart rate or respiration. Part of the responsibility of the SNS is preparing the body for stressful or dangerous situations and our 'fight/flight' response, which is our automatic physiological response to a situation or event we perceive as stressful.

In situations such as an identity crisis (when we find ourselves anxious and under threat), the SNS kicks in to enable you to leap into action. The SNS slows down bodily processes that are less important in emergencies, such as digestion, and pumps blood to the areas of our body that need more oxygen. This includes the heart, so that it can beat faster to improve the delivery of oxygen to parts of the body that need it under threat, such as our muscles that are needed to move away from the threat. This all happens without conscious thought and occurs automatically within the body.

The PNS is often referred to as the 'rest and digest' system as it functions to conserves the body's natural energy so it can be used later. It helps you to relax and rest, regulates bodily functions like digestion and urination and relaxes the body by lowering blood pressure, slowing or heart rate and breathing once a stressful situation or threat has passed. The PNS leads to decreased arousal and, the more time we spend with the PNS activated, the better we feel and healthier we are. Most relaxation techniques such as controlled breathing, meditation, massage, talking therapies, exercise and yoga aim to stimulate the PNS.

The SNS works alongside the PNS to maintain homeostasis, which is essential for survival and well-being and for the body to function correctly. Homeostasis involves balancing all the body's internal physiological mechanisms and maintaining that equilibrium.

If our internal states are out of balance, the body tries to return itself to equilibrium. It naturally wants comfort and relaxation. So, the SNS fires up the hormones epinephrine and norepinephrine (fight/flight response) that focus us, creating energy for action enabling us to push through to our end goal of regaining equilibrium.

As you make changes on your way to creating your new life, learning how to stimulate your own PNS can help you feel calmer and push through new situations which make you anxious.

Here are three techniques to help trigger your PNS.

Controlled breathing

People often breathe in shallow or restricted ways when they are under stress. If they feel particularly under threat, panicked, or stressed then their breathing can become faster or harder and they may begin to hyperventilate. Hyperventilation plays a significant role in most anxiety attacks. Controlled breathing is one way to counteract the symptoms of shallow, restricted or rapid breathing.

When your breathing is out of sync it upsets the delicate balance between oxygen and carbon dioxide in the brain. Subtle changes can offset this balance and result in unpleasant symptoms, including shortness of breath and feeling like you can't get enough air into your lungs; stomach pains; sweating; tingling face, hands or limbs; pain or tightness in your chest; muscle tremors or cramps; dizziness and visual problems; exhaustion and feelings of fatigue.

Learning to breathe slowly and deeply is a technique that will send a signal to activate your PNS enabling your body to begin to feel calmer, safer and soothed. Controlled breathing may take time and practice to become used to – but with practice, it can help you to become calmer in anxious times.

You can correct over-breathing and implement slow deep breathing by learning to breathe gently, slowly and evenly, in through your nose, filling your lungs completely, and then exhaling slowly and fully.

You can sit or lie down to practice this exercise. Breathe slowly and smoothly.

- Place one hand on your chest and one on your stomach.

- Breathe in through your nose and notice your hand move outwards as your lower belly expands. Count 1-2-3-4 to allow your lungs to fully fill with air. Keep your shoulders relaxed and try to keep your chest movement to a minimum.

- Now breathe slowly and evenly out through your nose as you count 1-2-3-4-5-6-7

- Slowly and evenly, breathe out through your nose. Count 1-2-3-4-5-6-7.

- Repeat. Ideally you should take eight to 12 breaths per minute. Try and get a steady rhythm going.

Progressive muscle relaxation

Stress can cause you to tense your muscles and a way to relieve muscle tension is by using progressive muscle relaxation exercises. In this technique, you tense up a particular group of muscles (for example the shoulder blades and the back) for approximately five seconds and then relax the muscles and keep them relaxed for approximately 10 seconds. Then you move onto the next set of muscles and consciously make your way around the whole body.

Guided imagery

This is an effective stress management and relaxation technique that can relax your body and your mind by imagining peaceful settings to reduce your own anxiety.

You can read or listen to a story like the following.

Imagine you are walking toward the ocean. You can hear the waves up ahead gently crashing onto the seashore. You can smell the sweet scent of the ocean spray. The air is warm and moist, and you can feel a cool breeze from the palm trees travelling across your face and shoulders.

You walk towards the ocean and come to the end of the palm trees, and you see the brilliant aqua colour of the sea and the glinting sparkle of the sun hitting the tops of the waves. There is a beautiful stretch of white sand just ahead of you and you slowly begin to saunter down it. The sand is powdery. Now imagine yourself taking off your shoes and letting your feet and toes relax into it as you gently lower your whole body onto the sand, feel the warmth of the sun on you and relax.

UNDERSTANDING AND MANAGING YOUR COGNITIVE RESPONSE TO ANXIETY

The cognitions we experience when we are anxious differ from those we experience with fear. With anxiety, our thoughts converge around not being able to control a possible threat and our inability to avoid, cope with or overcome the consequences of that threat. We might question how capable we are in midlife of letting go of core beliefs, people and objects, and worry about other changes we need to make, so it's essential, therefore, to keep our thoughts in check so we don't heighten our perception of those threat levels and induce even further anxiety.

If we recognise there is no threat, then we can reduce our anxiety. Similarly, if we feel we have the capacity to cope with the threat, then anxiety is reduced. If there is an actual threat and we know we won't be able to cope, then we experience fear.

Cognitive behaviour therapy (CBT) provides a framework in which to understand the impact of thoughts on our feelings and behaviours.[18] CBT is based on the assumption that the way we think about things affects the way we feel about them. CBT recognises that often we have ways of thinking which are unhelpful and can make us feel anxious.

It is a therapy approach that can help us to identify our anxious thoughts and challenge them to help us come up new, with more helpful thoughts which reduce anxiety.

To tackle anxious thoughts, it is important to identify them and change them by collating evidence that contradicts the thought which in turn reduces anxiety.

Identifying anxious thoughts and thinking errors

Certain common thinking errors can affect our well-being, increase anxiety and limit our lives and potential. Here are some common examples:

All or nothing thinking: 'This is the only relationship that will ever make me happy'. In this type of thinking, you are either a success or a failure – there's nothing in-between.

Always or never thinking: 'I will never get over this feeling of emptiness'. In this type of thinking, you see things in extreme, absolutist terms.

Mind reading: 'People must think I'm really stupid'. In this type of thinking you assume what others think of you without necessarily having any evidence.

Fortune telling: 'There's no point doing that, it'll never work'. In this type of thinking you can predict a negative outcome without considering the odds of it happening, jumping to conclusions instead.

Magnification: 'This one little mistake has ruined absolutely everything'. In this type of thinking, known as the binocular effect, the significance of a situation tends to be blown out of proportion.

Dwelling on the negative: 'If only I'd said that in the meeting'. In this type of thinking it's common to disregard any good things that might have happened and concentrate solely on any bad aspects of a situation.

Minimising the positive: 'I'm good at my job but anyone can do that'. In this type of thinking there is a downplaying of any positive aspects of a situation.

Catastrophising: 'My last relationship didn't work out, I'll never find love'. In this type of thinking people predict the worst-case scenario.

Self-blame and being over-responsible: 'She looks cross, it must be because of me'. In this type of thinking you assume responsibility for anything that goes wrong, even when it's not your fault. Responsible, hard-working people tend to do this.

Should and must statements: 'I should have my life in order by now'. In this type of thinking your thoughts can bury you in shame.

Emotional reasoning: 'I feel selfish when I prioritise myself, so I must be a really selfish person'. In this type of thinking your emotional reaction is assumed to be the truth.

These thinking errors provide a quick way to sabotage yourself and feel bad about yourself. It can be hard to move forward when you feel down, depressed and useless as a result of these unhelpful ways of thinking.

Challenging thoughts, gaining perspective, and generating alternative viewpoints

It is important to separate yourself from the thought – almost like an out-of-body experience where you stand back from the thought and see it as an individual thing. Consider:

- Whose voice is this? Is it useful?
- What is the nature of this thought? (e.g. catastrophising, magnification)
- What is the evidence that this thought is a fact?
- What is the contrary evidence?
- What would I tell a friend if they had the same thought?
- What would a friend say about this thought?
- Would I say what I am saying to myself to a friend who needed support?
- Am I being kind and compassionate to myself?
- Is my thought based on the way I feel, or based on facts?
- Am I totally condemning myself based on a single event?
- Can I identify other people, organisations or circumstances who may have played a part in this event?
- Am I becoming my thoughts (emotional reasoning)?
- Am I overestimating the chances of disaster?
- Am I committing myself to a 'should and must' situation instead of accepting and dealing with the reality of the situation?
- Am I assuming I can do nothing to change my situation?
- Am I predicting the future negatively by fortune telling, instead of experimenting with it, trying new things, and daring to even be excited by it?

And finally...

- What would be a far more helpful thought for me to have about this?
- Who or what (person/circumstance/situation) would support me in moving forward in my life?

Anxious thoughts – Kyle's story

Kyle's father had been a workaholic – everything stopped for work. In his 40s, when Kyle felt tired, he began to pull back from work. Kyle was a freelance journalist and wanted to work part-time, but his father had been in the military and berated anyone who did not work hard. Kyle wanted to pursue his love of writing and finish off the novel he had been working on for several months but struggled to find the time to finish. He reduced his hours and began to spend time on his own writing projects. He felt anxious all the time, thinking he should be working harder, and telling himself he was lazy.

In therapy we explored how his father's upbringing and how joining the forces had enabled him to gain some control in the chaotic home he was brought up in. His father's need to be busy had kept him out of the path of his angry alcoholic father. Kyle recognised this was not his experience and so did not have to apply his father's coping techniques to his life. He began to challenge the continuous negative thoughts he had that he was being lazy and self-indulgent, and also worked part-time. We talked through how being self-compassionate can be motivational and not a sign of weakness or letting yourself off the hook. He replaced his negative thoughts with more compassionate ones, such as, 'I am not hurting anyone by concentrating on my writing. I have needs and ambitions which are different to my father's, which is okay. My experience of life is different to my father; we are 30 years apart so, of course, we won't see eye to eye on how to live our lives'. These new thoughts allowed him to slow down in a more contented way and concentrate on being the person he wanted to be so he could be happier in his life. He worked on his self-compassion and allowed himself to enjoy his free time, which he actually spent very productively by choice.

The value of self-compassion

Self-compassion is the key to enabling us to self-soothe and help trigger our PNS. In midlife, your inner critic can often criticise you for not knowing and tell you you're making a drama about everything or being lazy and just looking for an excuse to do nothing. Quietening down the inner critic and finding an internal compassionate companion can reduce anxiety symptoms.

Compassion flows in three different ways. The compassion we offer to others, the compassion we receive from others and then the compassion we offer to ourselves – the latter is known as self-compassion.

Self-compassion is essential for change and an important predictor of well-being and resilience.[19][20][21] And we are going to need to be resilient in midlife if we are going to create a world around us in which we can live and thrive. There's a lot to do!

Research shows treating yourself compassionately when experiencing personal suffering promotes your mental health and has consistently been associated with lower levels of depression and anxiety.[22]

Self-compassion is a way of treating yourself with care in situations that are challenging or painful. If you tend to become overly critical of yourself when the going gets tough and feel you are failing or falling short of what is required of you, then be kind to yourself. Self-kindness is a way of caring and supporting yourself rather than attacking yourself for any perceived or real shortcomings.

It is all too easy to be self-critical in midlife especially if we are not living the life we want or after taking responsibility for getting ourselves stuck in a life that doesn't fit.

But it is really common that people have an inner critic or internal voice or monologue that criticises them in situations that are not ideal. It is possible, however, to develop a more measured approach and to speak to yourself compassionately and gently while also holding yourself responsible if needs be and looking at a way of moving forward.

While acknowledging that some things we have done have not been that helpful to us and need adjusting, it is okay to still look after ourselves as we start to change and learn from past mistakes. We do not need to beat ourselves up. There is growing evidence to support how being compassionate is far more effective in achieving your goals than being self-critical.

The danger of self-criticism

In my experience, many people are self-critical because at some level they believe that self-criticism will motivate them. They believe the alternative is to be kind to themselves and if they are too kind to themselves they will be self-indulgent, lazy, and underachieving. They will let themselves off the hook by making it okay to make mistakes and therefore reduce the quality of their work and friendships. When we look at how children respond to new, tricky, or challenging situations, it is easier to see how gentle encouragement amid mistakes can motivate them to keep on going rather than being critical and making them feel shame, which may result in them giving up. So it is with us.

Self-criticism can be destructive, undermine our motivation, and threaten our self-concept. If our stress response is constantly activated, we overproduce cortisol. For example, getting criticised at work can activate our stress response and then we attack ourselves with self-criticism – now we are both the attacker and the attacked – a double whammy! When we criticise ourselves, our body goes into threat mode, activating our SNS which releases adrenaline and cortisol as we prepare for the fight or flight response.

If you are a constant self-critic, you will have constant levels of high stress, and so the body will begin to shut down to protect itself, becoming slower and more susceptible to health conditions, such as depression, anxiety, and sleep problems. In time, overall performance will decrease too.

But self-compassion stops this damning cycle. Research shows that when we give ourselves compassion and speak kindly to ourselves, we release oxytocin and reduce our cortisol levels. Compassion activates our PNS. And when we feel safe and comforted, we can function well and be available to ourselves and to others – the opposite of being selfish.

With self-compassion, you give yourself the same kindness, care, and concern you would give to a friend. Imagine if a friend said 'I'm worried about my health. I'm exhausted, I'm worried I'm missing things at work, and my home life is breaking down'. You wouldn't say 'Oh for goodness' sake, you're so weak! Get a grip.' Or at least I hope you wouldn't. You might say 'You are doing the best you can under difficult circumstances, keep going, my friend' – a compassionate, kind response.

It is essential to become aware of how you treat yourself when you are suffering. Remember that self-compassion can help midlifers to pursue new goals and new experiences, which can be challenging and a bit frightening.

Lack of Self-compassion – Amanda's story

Amanda was an office manager. When her staff were struggling, she always met with them on an individual basis to talk them gently through their difficulties and offered support, taking into account their personal circumstances and capabilities.

When Amanda's midlife struggles took hold, her long-term relationship broke down. Also, her elderly mother, who she was very close to, was diagnosed with dementia and so Amanda had to take time off work to settle her into a nursing home. Amanda criticised herself for not coping well and did not extend any of the compassion and understanding she afforded her staff to her own personal circumstances. Her inner critic had an absolute field day!

'Is this all you can manage? Why are you grieving for the loss of a partner that you had outgrown anyway? You're letting your colleagues down.'

Amanda's self-compassion was non-existent. This lack of self-compassion is prevalent in most clients I see at the start of their therapy journey. To be kind to the self does not seem to come naturally at all to most people. It has to be consciously learned.

We explored what Amanda would say to one of her staff who was going through the devastating personal journey she was currently experiencing. She said she would be encouraging towards them saying, 'The fact you are still functioning with all this stress is amazing.' She acknowledged the stark contrast between what she would say to them and what she was saying to herself.

Amanda didn't need to stay long in therapy because she immediately began to challenge and change her self-talk, so she could function well and be motivated to look after herself and get back to work so she could look after others.

To increase self-compassion, it is essential to keep an eye (and ear) on what you're saying to yourself – your internal monologue.

Watch your internal monologue

Consider what you criticise yourself for the most. Recognise the internal monologue you give yourself – the specifics of the critique – 'I am lazy, I am fat, I am not interesting'. Now think about a time that was difficult for you or when you felt hurt or overlooked. What did you say to yourself? Were you caring and compassionate, as you might be towards a friend in a similar circumstance or was your critical voice pretty ruthless? Did it deny you any motivational dialogues? Did it just shame you more? Be gentle with yourself.

Watch out for negative thoughts that are one-sided, without a hint of anything positive. Common negative thoughts can centre around catastrophising the situation and minimising any good aspects. They can also be quite absolute, with a hint of mind reading such as 'this will never be any better'. Challenge the thoughts and find a gentler and kinder way to speak to yourself. Let yourself off the hook for insignificant things you've done wrong or would have preferred to have done better. Be less judgemental with yourself and more encouraging.

Get perspective. Perspective and alternative viewpoints to critical and shaming thoughts are helpful here. Also, getting opinions from, and spending time with your friends with, similar and complementary viewpoints and ways of being in the world like yours will help strengthen you. We would often we would never say to friends the harsh things we say to ourselves.

Find a new way to be gentle with yourself. Start with a reassuring voice, gentle tone and patient dialogue that you might use with a friend or loved one in distress. Use less shaming language and try to be more understanding of any challenges you might be struggling with. Try using these techniques for the next week.

UNDERSTANDING AND MANAGING YOUR BEHAVIOURAL RESPONSE TO ANXIETY

The behaviours experienced with anxiety are typically those of avoidance and withdrawal or keeping busy and not stopping. This might involve distracting yourself with pleasurable activities such as sex or spending money, being overly dependent on someone else to help reduce your anxiety or disengaging from a stressful situation or turning your attention elsewhere. You might also find yourself stuck in behavioural patterns of ruminating over and over the same thoughts.

Perhaps you have been side-stepping the unhappiness in your life through avoidance or by distracting yourself by doing fun things to occupy your mind. It stops you thinking of aspects of your life that make you unhappy. These passive coping strategies might work for a while, you think you are coping because your immediate anxiety and stress levels are reduced. In reality, the more an issue is not tackled the greater the build-up of anxiety and stress can be.

Passive coping examples might include:

- Refusing to call somebody back or answer an email because it triggers painful emotions in you that you don't want to feel.
- Putting things off because you don't want to acknowledge the truth – such as asking a friend if your behaviour has been unreasonable when you know that it has.
- Withdrawing from people or situations that are painful reminders that you are not living the life you desire for yourself, or that reinforce your current sadness.
- Using addictive behaviours such as drugs, alcohol, sex, porn or food to anaesthetise unwanted feelings, and avoiding dealing with the underlying issue.
- Spending money on treats for yourself such as a car or a holiday, which distract you away from your problems.
- Keeping your family life busy and active to avoid having to spend time with your partner one on one when you know there are problems between you.

These examples are unhealthy passive coping strategies because you are not directly facing and dealing with a situation or issue but avoiding or distracting from it instead.

When is avoidance coping okay?

Passive coping can be turned into active coping strategies that can be healthy and effective to manage emotions in the short and longer term.

In midlife, sometimes you can knowingly avoid a confrontation or situation because you are preparing to deal with it, but you're not ready to just yet. For example, you are unhappy with a situation at work but choose to ignore it because you are in the process of securing another job elsewhere. Or you consciously avoid an argument with your partner because you are in therapy working to understand where your relationship has gone wrong. Perhaps you are learning how to manage your bodily responses to anxiety through exercise, yoga class or relaxation in preparation for a situation you will be tackling soon which will raise your anxiety levels and symptoms.

In these situations, you are aware of your avoidance and acknowledge you are using a short-term avoidance strategy but recognise that there is a much bigger issue to be tackled when your resources for doing so are in place.

8

LIMINALITY

Once the impasse has been acknowledged, and you have let go of unhealthy attachments holding you back, you enter liminality.

The word liminality is derived from the Latin word limen, meaning threshold. The liminal space is a transitory space, the space a person occupies as they change from one situation or perspective to another – it is an emergent, unstable 'in-between' space in which the person may oscillate between hanging on to old identities because of the comfort they provide despite being outdated and reaching out into an unknown, new space that is yet to be fully formed.

There is no simple passage through the space here and you can feel a sense of social isolation as you traverse this very personal journey alone. Not everyone is as lucky as Dante, who had Virgil as his guiding companion through his midlife journey.

Here at the threshold of betwixt and between, we know we can no longer go back to being the person we used to be. We know that just doesn't work for us any more, but we don't yet know who we are trying to become. We don't know exactly what we are going to change, or the new choices we will make for ourselves. For many midlifers this situation can generate a strong feeling of being lost.

In 1969, Victor Turner said that liminality 'involves letting go of previously held views, attitudes, and status, and being prepared to reconsider and recalibrate. It means living life as transitional, in between, taking nothing for granted, recognising oneself perpetually at a crossroads, reconsidering choices'.[23]

It can feel like you are 16 years old again, on the threshold of adulthood, and letting go of the comfort, protection and lack of responsibility of childhood as you reach out and explore something new. This sense of the in-between can be very destabilising and anxiety-provoking – it can be unpleasant not knowing who you are and not having a formed identity. Yet do not despair. This is a normal process and all part of establishing a life worth living.

How we get through this liminal space is by acknowledging the liminal space, soothing ourselves to manage the anxiety, creating choices, listening to our body and monitoring and noting its response to change.

The liminal space can create a sense that you are 'floating'.[24] In liminality you are neither part of the old nor part of the new yet, and there is a sense that you are suspended in time, waiting for something. Of course, nothing happens externally yet, as all the change is internal in the form of new thoughts, curiosity, and self-awareness.

It can help to have company and understanding in this part of your transitional process, with people who are sharing the same liminal passage. Research shows there can be a heightened sense of belonging and togetherness in sharing this space with other like-minded people who can relate to this experience.[25]

Turner[26] coined the word 'communitas' to describe the special bond between those who share the same liminal passage, saying that this unique community continues even after the liminal period has concluded. The definition of communitas, which is a Latin noun, is the sense of belonging and sharing that develops amongst people who are experiencing liminality.

With this in mind, I set up a support and discussion group on Facebook called The Midlife Crisis Handbook Support Group. The group provides a safe, supportive space for people who understand the notion of liminality, the feelings that accompany an identity crisis and the sense of existing betwixt and between.

THE MAIN CHALLENGE IN LIMINALITY

Liminality can be a challenging space and one of emotional instability. It is a contemplative process involving reflection and reflexivity as we are yet to have all the answers. In this space over time, things will become clear and new lives and possibilities will begin to emerge. Liminality provides the spark of creation, the opportunity for new choices that can release you from old ties and allow you to embrace new-found freedom. It is a space where deep healing and transformation can take place – if you can tolerate the not knowing.

Liminality that is embodied and experienced within a life transition is temporary in nature, although it may last for an extended period of time. It is part of the transformational process. We can't rush the true process, but as many people (including my clients) like strategies, I have created a toolkit – not to rush you through liminality, but to gently stimulate thought processes and awareness and guide you along, so you can feel like you are 'doing' but essentially you are 'being'.

ESSENTIAL TOOLS FOR LIMINALITY

Changing your mindset about time

In midlife, people begin to focus on the limitations of the second half of their life – realising that life isn't forever, and often a sense that time is running out can begin to develop. Questions arise such as:

- Do I have enough time to change?
- How long are these changes going to take?

There's a sense that time is key, and that it is limited. This causes challenges for midlifers. It can be very tempting to implement a massive immediate overhaul of your life when you realise how you have been living. However, trust me when I say this is too much too soon. Decisions, actions, and behaviours carried out without self-awareness and from a panicky place can mean you end up right back at square one.

So, breathe. You have time to make the changes you need to make. Let's just be as certain as we can be that they are the right changes, those that will benefit you the most.

Our subjective sense of time plays such an important part in midlife and in personal motivation. If we feel that time is running out and that our future is limited, this can reduce our choices, making us reluctant to start new projects or to see through an idea that might lead to something fulfilling. If you can broaden your perspective on time, it will help negate the potential trade-off you might make if you rush to change things quickly. Time is a precious resource and an essential contributor to happiness. How people spend their time can greatly impact their well-being.

When we are younger, we set goals that are focused on expanding knowledge or goals that need time for us to research and collect information about. Time was generally experienced as open-ended. There was time enough to take a gap year, study for a part-time qualification over several years or go out with different people and explore your sexuality.

As we get older, our perception of time becomes more constrained. We tend to prioritise goals in terms of how quickly they can be achieved. In turn that prioritises our current emotional state and our sense of well-being, rather than expanding our horizons as it did when we were younger.

We plan to immediately relieve those emotional states we would prefer not to experience, such as anxiety. We dislike our jobs, so we shift companies; we are unhappy in our relationships, so we have an affair or leave to bring some fun into our life; we feel depressed, so we see the doctor and are prescribed antidepressants – all in an attempt to alleviate the feelings we don't want to feel. It's hard to experience uncomfortable emotions, but in midlife a shift in time and perspective is needed. Pausing, and being able to tolerate the emotions we don't want, will allow us to consider our next move and can help to ensure we address not only the physiological symptoms but also the cause of our distress.

Gauging your perception of time

If you feel that your time is constricted, then you feel rushed. You might feel you don't have enough time to make necessary changes, so will have to compromise, which will then impact and compromise your life decisions.

Elongating your perception of time can have numerous positive effects. If you've ever had bad news delivered to you, or been in an accident, or tripped and fallen, you may have experienced a sense of time standing still or moving slowly. As we grow older, we can experience a sense of time whizzing by: here we are at Monday again! There seems to be no definitive research or explanation of why time seems to speed up as we get older. What I do know is that in my experience, people make better choices – those that are more worthwhile, fulfilling, and meaningful – when they don't exclude options because they will take longer to complete.

As Goethe said, 'We always have time enough, if we will but use it aright'.

Yes, you could take a short course in computer programming at a local college, but if this is truly your passion, why not enrol in a part-time degree, because in three years' time you could have a new career that could capture your interest through to retirement. You could do a six-week coaching course on salsa, but what if you chose a year-long course on modern ballroom dancing and begin to enter competitions and socials, meeting people with similar interests? You're unhappy at work, but you stay and negotiate new terms for your job. You're unhappy in our relationship so you both go and see a professional counselling and make the time to work through the difficulties you are experiencing. You feel depressed so you join a running club and start to eat healthily and give up alcohol.

Gaining a sense that you have time could transform your decision-making and the quality of your life.

Research[27] suggests that in many cultures we are led to believe that money cultivates happiness, but what actually increases happiness is how we spend our time. This research shows that a person's sense of the amount of time they have available to them is a clear indicator of health and well-being, while ailments such as poor sleep, headaches, hypertension, and stomach pain can all be linked to the feeling that time is constricted. So, if we could change our perspective towards time and, as Goethe suggests, spend it in the right way, then there is every chance that our subjective well-being would improve.

It's important that time is spent increasing personal meaning and connectedness. In a research article entitled 'If money doesn't make you happy, consider time'[28] it is suggested that to get maximum happiness out of time, people need to use it in ways that cultivates personal meaning and social connections.

The following ways of spending time (which costs nothing) would increase our well-being:

- spend time with the right people – interactions associated with the greatest happiness levels tend to be friends, family, and significant others, whereas bosses and co-workers tend to be associated with the least happiness.[29]
- spend time on the right activities – those that cultivate meaning, such as socially connecting activities and helping someone else.
- enjoy the experience without spending the time – spend time thinking about happy memories. Sometimes the anticipation of something can be more pleasurable than the actual event, so

enjoy time with pleasant thoughts in the run-up.
- expand your time – achieved by living in the present moment and taking stock as you go.
- be aware that happiness changes over time – be flexible because how you enjoy your time may change as life changes – go with it.

Exercise 12: Perception of time

How would you act differently today if you had all the time in the world that allowed you to recover emotionally from events and retrain and start again? How would you change your...

- primary relationship?
- career?
- social life?
- skill set?
- hobbies?

How would answers to the above differ if you had six months to live?

If your answers are different, it will be worth asking yourself whether you can invest in yourself and your precious time for the longer term. This would yield truly meaningful results rather than less time-consuming achievements and goals that might work in the short term, but lose their appeal if you live another 30 years.

The power of stopping, pausing, space and silence

There is power in doing nothing and holding the tension in life before moving forward. Waiting for true, sustainable interest and enthusiasm for a change of life, pace, relationship or career can take time. The challenge is to wait it out while increasing self-awareness and identifying your true needs and wants. That way, longer term decisions are made that really connect to the true midlife self. This way of being directly challenges how so many of us make decisions too quickly to reduce the anxiety of indecision and inevitably end up repeating old patterns in our life.

The empty space you create by stopping and not proceeding immediately is often the most challenging part for my clients to embrace. Many of my clients are good at 'doing', so getting them to stop and self-reflect is often their biggest challenge. It is important to reflect on where you have been and where you might be going. This can be uncomfortable and drive you a little stir-crazy because there is no outward movement. But pausing does involve inward movement, which is far more valuable at this stage of a midlife transition.

I encourage my clients to stop. Stopping is usually much harder for people because it's easier to jump on to the next project without really thinking. Of course, this helps stave off thoughts of being lazy, unproductive and time-wasting. Invariably things won't change unless you take a different approach to improving your life and happiness. Remember, the definition of insanity is doing the same thing over and over and expecting different results.

Allow yourself time to really contemplate the future that you desire. Use self-compassion to support yourself emotionally while you wait for true interest, passion and vitality to arise. It's no different to the teenage years – we form our sense of self over time, not based on snap decisions – so don't start now.

In midlife, many of us are crying out for stillness and silence within our lives and within our culture. I know many midlifers have a powerful urge to shut themselves off, disappear quietly on their own or run away. What are we seeking, what are we searching for? The world isn't going to change for us, we are not going to become a culture of inner reflection and quiet times any time soon, so it is essential that we provide this for ourselves.

The author Lori Deschene encouraged the concept of practising the pause by developing pausing as a skill to use before further actions or thoughts. She said, 'Practice the pause. Pause before judging. Pause before assuming. Pause before accusing. Pause whenever you're about to react harshly and you'll avoid doing and saying things you'll later regret'.[30]

Use the pause as a way of creating a space to become aware before action.

Techniques employed with my clients typically have included:

- Writing a gratitude list before responding. Consider all the good things in your life, and what you're grateful for, and write it down.

- Writing down in your journal how you would like to react and the possible consequences of doing this. This will increase self-awareness.

- Waiting before responding and during this time, trying to understand the other person's point of view, their argument, and their motivation for having this stance, before you consider sharing yours.

- Keeping an eye on your negative thoughts, challenge them and also use self-compassion and engage your PSN to help with the physiological effects of anxiety overwhelm.

- Writing a gratitude list before responding. Consider all the good things in your life, and what you're grateful for, and write it down.

Changing your mindset about space

The fertile void – allowing space between our old and new selves.

As we now know, one inevitable consequence of a midlife crisis or a life transition is a sense of being lost, not really knowing how we want to be or what to do for the best. To support clients in this liminal space I use the psychological concept of 'the fertile void' developed by Gestalt therapist Fritz Perls[31] as it helps them in altering their perspective of the unknown, helping them to reconfigure it – see it through a different lens.

Entering a midlife crisis where old identities no longer fit, and a new identity has yet to be formed, creates a void that leaves an emptiness and a 'not knowing' that requires you to look inward in order to move through it. There is without doubt a gap between your old identity and the formation of your new one, which is unsettling. However, if you can view this gap as a fertile space – a space of renewal and new growth and new opportunities, this can take some of the panic out of it.

Clarkson[32] described the void as 'the emptiness through which we all must pass as we let go of one set of experiences in order to fully engage with a new set of experiences'. Within that 'lost' space, the fertile void harnesses the idea that, in order for something to flourish and evolve, an empty space needs to be created. It encourages us to refigure the unknown, to stop and reflect on our lives – the good, the bad, and the ugly – and wait a while before we continue on our way.

This can be a very useful way of giving permission for space for people who like to keep busy because it is a productive strategy for personal growth and keeps the 'I'm being lazy' thoughts at bay!

Stepping into the void can be frightening because, when we enter it, we don't have all the answers. We don't know where we are going to end up. Our direction is unclear. If you can manage the anxiety of not knowing and the feeling of overwhelm, then the void will allow your true energy to rise without it having to be forced. Your vitality and passion for life will then re-emerge alongside. Chances are this will mean a change of direction for you and a time of adjustment, positivity and real growth.

Exercise 13: The fertile void

Using the concept of the fertile void – allowing space between our old and new self- consider the following questions. Make a note of anything that occurs to you, or where you sense you would like to spend more time contemplating.

What or who do I need to help me feel nourished in this space? (e.g. alone time, solitude, being with others)	
What do I need to pay attention to?	
What new ideas emerge within this space that I need to cultivate?	

Allowing yourself to pause means that, inevitably, something will shift. It's the quality of the shift we are interested in – it isn't about quickly moving on, it is a quiet contemplation and awareness of the situation that impacts the quality of the shift.

9

STRATEGIES TO GUIDE CHANGE

YOU HAVE CREATED SOME SPACE, slowed down your own life transition and taken yourself out of panic mode. Now the possibility of informed change arises. There are different ways to spark creative thinking; you can use your body; you can think about change, or even access your inner voice to offer guidance. See which option suits you best.

USING THE BODY AS A GUIDE

The mind and body are intertwined in the same way as our physical and emotional health. But we tend to neglect the body as an indicator of emotional health. Often, our body isn't noticed until it stops functioning, or fatigue or low mood makes it difficult for us to function.

We might notice more obvious physical signs, like butterflies in the stomach or an increased heartbeat when we are excited, tension headaches, hot flushes, heaviness or slowing down when we are low in mood.

In my experience, the body doesn't lie and is often well ahead of cognitive or intellectual thoughts. So, when a client comes to therapy having just recently been offered a promotion yet finds it hard to arrive at the office on time, be enthusiastic with colleagues, or fight off feelings of lethargy, I know that their body is telling them something. The promotion might make sense intellectually, but their somatic (bodily) reactions need attention.

In this particular case, the hesitancy of the body and its reluctance to 'turn up' had to be considered and listened to – perhaps it was saying, 'The promotion isn't for you'. Perhaps the body was keen to take the client down an alternative path, one that they haven't recognised as more interesting. Perhaps this promotion compromised their values and would take them higher up a corporate ladder that was pitched against the wrong wall.

Using your body to consider how you are being impacted by your environment or people when you are trying our new ways of being can be useful. Using the body as a guide takes people out of their heads, which is handy because often midlife crises can make no logical sense as all seems well on paper. So why not use awareness, energy and your visceral responses as a gauge. When you are unsure of the changes you need to make and can't come to a decision, it can be beneficial to try a different approach and ask your body.

We can't always articulate what we want, or see a clear end goal, so as an alternative to start making changes, I recommend using your body and your feelings as a way of determining whether changes you are considering feel like they are setting you off on the right path. Do they resonate with how you believe you want to live your life?

Try and identify your bodily reaction and feelings you experience when you consider and carry out change in your life. Use this process:

- Noticing. You become interested in trying or doing something new. This might be joining a new social group, dating someone new, ending a relationship, or wanting to speak to your boss about something. Try to notice physical sensations such as excitement, interest, energy, warmth, increased breathing or fatigue in your body when you have been stimulated by the prospect of this change. Note, too, how your body reacts when you are interested or curious about a conversation or story or something you have seen or read, or a new idea, or the prospect of doing something different in your life.

- Identify the feelings you're having and the thoughts that accompany them such as, 'this feels exciting', 'this feels right', or 'this fills me with dread'.

- Energy. The more you consider making this change, track the energy levels in your body. Do you continue to feel excited a few days later? Are you researching ideas relating to the change or speaking to others about it, seeking guidance and searching the internet to see if and how other people have done similar things? Does your body want to push forward with this idea for change?

- Action. When you implement the change and create the potential for something new to happen in your life, how do you feel? Does your body feel lighter? Does it feel like something has shifted inside of you?

Anxiety and excitement have very similar physiological effects on the body. If you are trying something new for the first time, you are likely to experience anxiety.

It can take time to work out if what you are feeling is a signal to stop or just a normal signal of stepping out of our comfort zone. Try to stand firm to allow time for you to understand your emotions.

Use relaxation exercises to manage these emotions and get support from friends.

Above all, check that the changes you are making are in line with your values and what you want for yourself.

The body keeps the score – Robert's story

Robert had wanted to be a firefighter since the age of 11. In his early 40s he had pursued a successful career as a firefighter, working his way up to station commander. He enjoyed his work but found himself increasingly reluctant to get up in the morning to go to work; he was fatigued and anxious. He came to therapy to address this.

He felt it was time to process his experiences as he'd never really stopped to consider the impact on himself. The years of rescuing people and seeing traumatic things had taken a toll and he was bordering on burnout. He also recognised that he was no longer the 18-year-old who joined the service looking for excitement and danger in his work. His body was tired and letting him know of the strain he was under, even though cognitively he felt he was still up to the job.

He knew he wanted to continue his career in public service so we started to consider different ways in which he could still serve but without the emotional toll. He stepped down as station manager and joined the human resources department, mentoring and training recruits. He felt this was more appropriate for his age and experience and a way of maintaining high standards for the next generation of firefighters.

DIVERGENT THINKING

New ways of thinking about yourself and your life and what you want can help push you along through liminality. Divergent thinking is the cognitive process of creating a new or different idea or approach to a problem that will advance your innovative skills and allow you to think outside the box. This style of thinking tends to be unpolished and random. It isn't easy moving through liminality, so a new set of skills can come in handy as a new method of problem-solving.

Divergent thinking works well when you have self-awareness. The previous exercises will have provided you with some clarity on an area of your life where you feel stuck – or maybe several areas. For now, just concentrate on one area. Hopefully, you will begin to recognise how your stuckness may be related to a way of living or thinking that no longer suits you or buys into someone else's way of living. Here are some short exercises to create new thoughts and strategies around the stuckness. These can be used for new actions and behaviours in the future.

Be clear about the area of your life you want to work on first. Clarify your main problem such as 'I'm unhappy in my work', or 'I'm bored, and the things I do no longer bring me joy', or 'I need a new social network', or even 'My marriage is over, I need to move on'.

- Brainstorming. This is a technique that lists as many ideas as possible within a short period of time – maybe two to five minutes. The ideas can be unstructured and just jotted down. The key tool here is called 'piggybacking', whereby you use one idea to stimulate a run of ideas off the back of it. Nothing at this stage is disregarded or criticised – it's a free-flowing exercise. Afterward, you can go back and review the ideas and consider and critique their value and merit before deciding if you want to take one or more of them forward in a more formalised way.

- Keep a journal. It is always handy to keep a journal close at hand and at the side of your bed at night to jot down anything you think of spontaneously – maybe when your thoughts have been stimulated by a dream, prompted perhaps by events during the day or by the behaviour of someone else, or by something unusual has grabbed your attention. Nowadays, people tend to make notes on their phones and these notes can be a source of information to use in liminality to stimulate ideas for a new way of being.

- Free association or free writing. This is a little different to brainstorming as it involves focusing on one topic and writing about it non-stop for a short period of time, maybe five minutes. Don't stop to think about what you are writing, don't correct spelling or grammar mistakes, and don't proofread your work – just let it flow out of you and onto the paper. The idea here is to generate a variety of thoughts about a topic and see how you 'talk' or write about it – the words you use, and the enthusiasm on the page. These thoughts can then be restructured and organised into more cohesive thought processes and full sentences later.

- Mind mapping. This involves putting all the ideas you have brainstormed down on paper in the form of a visual map or picture and then connecting the thoughts to show the relationships between them. You'll need to start with a central idea or question and write it in the middle of the paper. Then any different aspects or facets of this idea are drawn branching off from this key idea – these are sub-topics that might well include sub-topics of their own.

  For example, career might be the key idea/issue you are concentrating on with a view to actioning later on – branching off from that might be a new area of interest. Let's say your career was financial services and your area of interest included buy-to-let housing, offshore investing, accounting, and economics. You expand your thoughts around buy-to-let housing to the two areas that resonate and excite you – student letting or shared housing for young professionals. An initial image is created off the central idea with branches of ideas off (subtopics) and then refining ideas of those branches (sub-topics of sub-topics). It would look something like this:

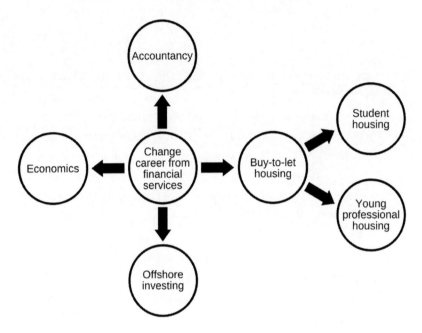

Add to the diagram as new topics of interest resonate positively with you so what starts out initially as a process of divergent thinking then switches to convergent thinking as you begin a narrowing down of thinking into a more exact thought or well-defined idea.

Exercise 14: Brainstorming

Now try the brainstorming and free association techniques and try to answer these questions related to the area of life you want to change:

What am I afraid to do?	
What might my most adventurous friend tell me to do?	
What would my mother/father/primary carer prefer me to do?	
If the outcome was guaranteed to be successful and I could get away unscathed, what would I do?	

SELF-GUIDANCE AND INNER WORK

Not everyone has support from others as they move through the liminal space. Many people will be invested in you not changing, and maintaining the status quo. If these previous strategies feel too linear for you, then consider more abstract concepts to generate new thoughts and ways of thinking.

Be your own guide

Carl Jung saw the psyche as a self-regulating system that was always striving for growth, In order to use the psyche as a guiding force, I ask clients to consider the prospect of a wise figure deep within the self.

As Dante encountered his midlife crisis in the Inferno, he was accompanied on the way by Virgil – his guide. I like the idea of company along a personal journey because otherwise it can feel very isolating and lonely. Rather than having a physical person, let us create a wise figure from within. This would be an inner voice, a compassionate friend who can accompany you throughout and beyond this transition: the voice you would offer to another. The voice of a compassionate friend could be based on a real person, living or dead, who had your best intentions at heart. It might be a character from a film who was caring and kind, or anyone you have experienced throughout your life as a positive, non-judgemental person.

Exercise 15: The inner guiding voice

Here we are going to travel within ourselves and ask questions that might encourage an inner voice to speak up on our behalf. See if you can answer the following questions:

What does the wise figure deep down inside of you tell or advise you to do?	
What do you already know deep down is inevitable but hasn't happened yet?	
Who were you meant to be?	
What action do you know deep down you must begin?	
Where in your life do you need to grow up?	
What would you like a fortune teller to say to you?	
What's the character trait that served you well in you youth that no longer works for you in midlife?	

Part 2: Working Out What You Want From Life

If you threw a coin into a wishing well, that would you wish for?	
What was the dream that died?	
When did you feel really alive and free?	
What's the story you're still believing about yourself that isn't true?	

The wise figure within – Joseph's story

Joseph had been emotionally neglected as a child. Both his parents had been alcoholics and had always prioritised their addiction over him and his siblings. Joseph grew up not always able to recognise his own needs. As such, he found it hard to know what he wanted in life, or from a relationship.

Joseph found self-compassion hard and so in therapy we found a different way that worked for him to access his needs. He kept a photo of himself as a six-year-old in his wallet to remind himself that he had a responsibility to look after the younger part of himself that had been so neglected. He found this easier than making himself the priority. Around the age of six, when he was being bullied at school, a kind teacher stepped in to support him emotionally and put a stop to the bullying. In therapy, when he had to consider what he really needed, he imagined this teacher asking him in a kind, gentle way what he needed for himself. This worked for Joseph.

WHY IS CHANGE SO HARD?

No matter how motivated we might feel, change can still be challenging and terrifying.

Whether it's in the workplace or the therapy room, one of the most demoralising things for an employee or client is when they become stuck. They are resistant to change and are unable to remove obstacles in their life that hinder growth and get in the way of their dreams, hopes and desires.

Let's consider what obstacles you might encounter along your midlife journey that might be holding you back from making changes.

Fear of failure

Robin Sharma[33] said, 'The project you are most resisting carries your greatest growth'. Why would this be the case? If it is the case, why don't we immediately get going and head to the finish? Fear comes in varying forms – fear of the unknown, fear of upsetting someone, fear of being seen as a lesser mortal by others, fear of being single, fear of becoming invisible, fear of consequences of actions or fear of failing. If we experienced only a little bit of worry, we'd probably have a go at change, as it's not too risky. But change can be a big worry, the potential risks profound, and that may prevent us from even trying.

We need to challenge the fear: is it really as catastrophic as we think it will be? Are we discounting our ability to explain our actions, to ask for help and support, to self-soothe and ride out the worry? Sometimes we imagine ourselves as helpless, as we were when we were younger, stuck at home with no agency or power to effect change in the world. But as adults we do have agency. We have agency over our thoughts and our ability to reach out for support from friends, family, written material, helplines or therapy. We can learn and practise techniques to change our catastrophic thoughts and challenge the validity of them.

Fear of Success

How can we be fearful of making a success of things? Marianne Williamson, a spiritual leader, author and lecturer, once wrote these famous words, 'Our deepest fear is not that we are inadequate. Our deepest fear is that we are powerful beyond measure. It is our light, not our darkness, that most frightens us'.[34]

It is often a fear of success rather than failure that keeps people trapped. If you haven't been brought up to enjoy and to embrace success, then the prospect of becoming successful could be daunting for you. To be successful or the star of the show can be anxiety-provoking, as you suddenly find yourself under the microscope with people watching and assessing your every move. Waiting in the wings and not changing, while ultimately less fulfilling, can feel like a much safer, less exposing option.

Consider embracing the success. It doesn't have to change you as a person, but you will have control over how you act and the extent to which you engage with others. Again, don't discount your ability to manage your own anxiety. Just make sure you are around supportive people who can help to ground you.

Secondary gains

These gains are the benefits or advantages that people experience by not changing. They are often not fully conscious thoughts. Often in therapy, when a client feels 'stuck' we examine what would be the consequences of change. For example, if you are depressed and your partner feels responsible for you and would never leave you while you are in this state, then this may offer you security within a relationship. If you were well, your partner might leave and then you'd have to take responsibility for yourself.

However, secondary gains can keep you stuck and reliant. It is only when the pain of not changing begins to outweigh the benefits of the secondary gain that we begin to liberate ourselves and move on. You may not have reached that stage yet – hence the lack of motion.

Lack of motivation to sustain change

We know that motivation is a powerful and valuable commodity. When it is lacking it can be hard to sustain interest and energy in getting things done or continuing with them. Deciding how to act and making informed changes that support your values means you are not forcing yourself to act. you are therefore more able to generate the energy to make change happen. This can happen while you establish the essentials of your new identity using values and motivation to drive you towards what you truly desire. In Exercise 2: Recognising my values (page 26), we looked at clarifying values. This is vital because now you can use your own values to leverage behavioural change. Being clear about your values will enable you to create choices that can lead to informed change, and ultimately to personal freedom and the path to a truer self.

Being unclear about your end goal

Often, the very nature of a life transition means that your end goal can feel unclear and unattainable. Generic midlife goals might be being true to yourself, increased peace of mind, feeling free, living authentically, or finding your purpose. Corporate-style goal setting doesn't really work here because if we could be specific and knew what we wanted at the end and knew how long it would take we could use the corporate goal-setting principles SMART (Specific, Measurable, Achievable, Relevant, and Time-Bound). However, we don't have the answers to these goal-setting parameters. So, why not use the body as your guide instead?

Part 2: Working Out What You Want From Life

SUMMARY

We've reached the end of Part 2. Having completed the exercises, I hope you will have increased your self-awareness and freed yourself up to let go of unhealthy attachments. You have explored some ideas about where you can find alternative support from a healthier source whether that be from others or from within yourself. You've also increased your understanding of any obstacles in your life which might stand in the way of any future change you'd like to make.

So, float in liminality for a while. Use your body, values, motivation, reduced anxiety, silence, pausing, new ways of thinking, to gently push yourself along. Already you may have a clearer idea about the potential changes you are considering that would move you further to your updated life goals, hopes, dreams, and desires. And so, my friend, it is time to move to Part 3 – action – gentle action – in the right direction – at last! It's time to recalibrate your life and create a new template for living in the now.

Part Three

RECALIBRATING THE NEW YOU

WORK
FINANCES
PLAY
SOCIAL
PARENTING
SPIRITUALITY
FAMILY
HEALTH
RELATIONSHIPS
SEX AND INTIMACY
JOY
SELF-ESTEEM
COMFORT IN LIFE
RELAXATION

RECALIBRATING THE NEW YOU

Jane Fonda said, 'It's never too late – never too late to start over, never too late to be happy.'[35]

I wholeheartedly agree.

So, let's get going! Let's recalibrate you!

To recalibrate means to change the way you think about something. In this context, it means reorganising, reshaping, and reinventing you and your world. This reinvention aims to increase your happiness by developing new meaning and purpose now that you have let go of rules that belong to other people. Those rules have limited your beliefs, restricted your potential and your attachments, and inhibited your personal growth. The first half of your life has been about fitting into the world – the second half is about creating a world that fits around you.

You won't always know where you are heading or what lies at the end of each new decision you make. But know this: you are unhappy, and change can be essential for happiness. You might deviate from your path, and you may not always make the right choices, but it's how quickly you can realign your way that counts.

Midlife goals are not always definable, and happiness isn't achieved by one singular event. If you can't reach a definable goal, I suggest living according to a theme of how you want to live. A theme is a guiding principle, your personal manifesto, based on your values and a declaration of how you want to live your life. It gives you opportunities for contentment every day, as your actions connect with what's important and essential for you. A theme is alive with an ongoing sense of meaning that underpins your choices and actions. It is a way to be content and satisfied in life and to acknowledge that you are good enough. It is an alternative to a goal which, if not achieved, can be demoralising and make you feel like a failure.

What will the theme of the second half of your life be? It can be a single word such as 'growth', 'kindness', or 'autonomy', or it can answer the question 'who do I want to be?' in ways such as:

- I want to be free.
- I want to be more me.
- I want to live a life that reflects my true self.
- I want to find peace of mind (this was what I personally wanted for myself).

Part 3 guides you as you reshape those aspects of your life that you identified as low in satisfaction in Exercise 1: The personal balance wheel (page 18). There might be a few areas of your life that scored low and therefore need recalibrating, but I suggest you concentrate on one area at a time. For each of the 14 areas below, I offer advice and action based on the most common midlife dilemmas and situations experienced to help you recalibrate this area of your life towards greater happiness. Some action points are repeated in more than one area of life because they contribute to overall wellbeing.

Your role through this next part of the book is to select an area of life you identified as being of low satisfaction and begin to recalibrate it. Habits that no longer support your personal growth may need to alter, the people you hang around with may begin to alter, you may change your workplace, revitalise old friendships, finally tackle unhealthy family dynamics or structure your life to include more play, fun and relaxation. Let's see.

As we begin to think about change, it is helpful to keep in mind the following tips.

- Take your time. Align your actions and choices based on self-awareness, current values and needs and how you want to live, rather than impulsive decisions.
- Trust your instincts. You may start down a path and then have a feeling or sense it's not quite right. Have you compromised yourself? Have you done something to please someone else and not been true to how you want to live? Recognise impor-

tant times in your decision-making, and consciously choose a path that supports your values to ensure the changes you make are in the right direction.

- Be selective. Keep the parts of your current life which connect and resonate with the true you and that you definitely want to keep. You don't have to change everything.
- Be flexible. The journey to change in midlife may not be linear and may have many twists and turns that you may not expect.
- Use the body as a guide. Tune into the feelings you have as you make changes. Try to distinguish good feelings such as natural excitement and nervousness from a sense of angst or discomfort that may accompany you if you force yourself to do something that doesn't fit with the life you want for yourself.

And so to action, or active experimentation, which means that we learn by doing.

WORK

The professional midlife crisis is a lot more widespread than people realise. Most people have financial commitments which limit their ability to leave a job they have outgrown, and others might be in a position to leave, or are working towards leaving, but are unsure what they want to do next.

For most of us, work takes up such an enormous part of our waking life that it is essential that we are happy in it, or else discontentment can easily spill into all the other areas of our life and lead to depression, relationship problems, sleep issues and burnout.

From my experience, midlifers have often been in their chosen profession for a couple of decades, sometimes longer, and have climbed well up the corporate ladder to professional success, yet are desperately unhappy, unfulfilled and bored. Others will have regularly changed from job to job, seeking out some satisfaction or a new challenge in their work. You might have made changes as a result of feeling undervalued, looking for a healthy work-life balance, exploring different careers trying to find what works for them, wanting better pay and benefits, more flexibility around juggling children and work hours, wanting to be your own boss, lack of trust in an organisation, wanting more fulfilment in work, or being headhunted. Many of my clients are in a relationship where their salary contributes to the couple's financial commitments, others are single and have a mortgage and other responsibilities which mean just quitting their job isn't an option.

There is no easy way out here, as responsibilities don't disappear overnight. Articles offering quick strategies for overcoming your professional midlife crisis are futile, as finding meaning in our professional life after it has been lost is not a quick fix. It requires conscious negotiation of choices and steady change as responsibilities continue to be upheld or re-negotiated.

A quick jump to a new position to feel like you are doing something positive can often be an attempt to immediately reduce current anxiety without full awareness of the core source of unhappiness. It usually provides only a temporary fix. When you're looking for fulfilment in our career, a thorough exploration and search of the exact elements of what you need in our job to make you happy is required. This enables you to consciously work towards true fulfilment.

With these scenarios in mind, here are some general action points to work out what is unsatisfactory in your current role followed by action points of other specific work situations:

- Clarify uncertainty. Be clear about what it is that doesn't work for you any more. What elements of your work support your well-being, and which detract? Consider both external or internal factors and how present your values are within your work.

    External factors are those stresses we are aware of around us, such as long hours, heavy workload, lack of breaks, lack of opportunity, poor management, organisational change and workplace bullying. These factors are difficult to change yourself and are dependent on collaboration with others. However, once the source of your unhappiness has been identified, consider if there is any flexibility or prospect of change in this element within the organisation. Would your ideas for change be considered or supported? If there is little chance of change, and if you decide to leave them, future employers would need to offer something different in this area which suits you better.

    Internal factors are negative self-talk, self-limiting beliefs, and unrealistic thinking and expectations – stresses that go on within you and cause unease. Stress from other areas of your life may also be making it difficult for you to enjoy your work. When it is your internal state of mind or dialogue which is contributing to your unhappiness, then the locus of control is internalised, and you can take responsibility and start to effect change rather than passively wait for change to happen to you. Consider how you can change these factors and look again at the anxious thoughts and thinking errors section in Chapter 7 (page 92). Consider coaching or counselling if you need more individual structured help.

- Stay true to your values. Remind yourself of the values you chose for yourself earlier in Exercise 2: Recognising my values (page 26) and consider how centred around your values your current work is. If there is no trace of these values within your work, that could explain any feelings of lack of purpose and meaning you might experience in the workplace.

  For example, if you chose sustainability as one of your main values and you are working for an organisation with a high carbon footprint or a heavy use of non-recyclable plastic, this will grate against your values and cause some internal conflict for you. Maybe it's the company's culture, staff members, ethical stance, workload, lack of appreciation or recognition from management or the promotion of a product or service you no longer see value in. If you chose personal growth as an important value, but you're in an industry with no prospect of promotion or with a glass ceiling or other invisible barriers preventing you from achieving further promotion or advancement, then you might be better off elsewhere.

TIME FOR TOUGH CONVERSATIONS

If some elements of work are working for you, and you want to stay in the job but recognised that changing certain things is important for you – then consider making your feelings and dissatisfaction known. Here are some action points:

- Speak up. Speak to your boss, human resources, a coach or a mentor to see if you can rejig this part of your working life in a more fitting and fulfilling way. Do your homework before the meeting and have a clear idea of how you would like to change your role and how it would benefit the company. If you want a pay increase, flexible hours or to be less micromanaged, then do explore these options and have all your reasons for requesting this at the ready. It's also important, when asking for a change in your work duties or conditions, to be honest and realistic with yourself about what you are actually prepared to do.

- Consider whether you are willing to go the extra mile and work longer hours for the promotion you're requesting or if you want to go part-time will you actually go back to college to study for further career progression. If you reduce your hours, are you realistically going to cut down on your outgoings? You'll be more motivated to go the extra mile if your changes align with your values.

WHEN LEAVING ISN'T AN OPTION

The last thing anyone needs when they have financial commitments is a sense that their job is unfulfilling, starting to drain them and it is becoming increasingly difficult to raise the energy to get out of bed each morning to go to work and be polite to work colleagues or the boss. Maybe you already feel trapped in the job by financial commitments but up until your crisis you've been able to push through and adequately bury your feelings of frustration and a desire for something more meaningful.

If you can't quit your job (e.g. for health insurance reasons, pension or financial commitments) there are other ways to make your working life better. Here are some action points to consider:

- Choose your colleagues carefully. As we spend so much time at work it can be important who we hang around with. Positive people with a healthy work ethic who are supportive and understanding of each other and your situation can help you to feel more motivated. Make the workplace more enjoyable with the quality of the contact you have in it. Equally, if there are people who drain you, it is okay to separate yourself.

- Set boundaries outside of work. Do you notice issues with your boundaries at work that are causing you unhappiness? You can tighten up your work boundaries by leaving on time and not discussing work once you leave the premises. Turning off notifications on your phone or email outside of set hours can give you defined quality time away from the organisation.

- Start a peer group. Starting a peer/social/support group within your workplace or from different organisations within your industry can help. Being around people who understand and empathise and can offer support can have a positive impact. Sharing common issues about challenges within the organisation or with customers can help normalise your situation and make you feel less like it's your issue and only you who with a problem.

    Conversations don't have to be centred around the unhappy things which are work-related but on supporting each other within the work environment, too. Gatherings work well when they are placed outside of the workplace such as in one person's home, or around an activity such as bowling, or meeting for a casual coffee. If you start the group, you can decide who can join and set the ground rules, such as limiting negativity and apportioning only part of the time together to talking about work issues.

- Specialise and become an expert. Consider specialising in one particular area of work which resonates with you. Becoming an expert in this one aspect of your job might help you to maintain interest and enthusiasm for the job and boost your self-esteem as you support others with your knowledge.

    Several years into my career, I researched and became knowledgeable about burnout and wrote and developed on-line courses on the subject. When I felt I had said everything I needed to say about burnout, I shifted my attention to midlife because I wanted to stay in psychology but knew I needed a different specialism to learn about and maintain my interest.

- Request reasonable adjustments. Throughout the world there are employment laws that oblige employers to make reasonable adjustments to accommodate requests for changed working conditions. You could consider asking for a flexible working schedule, at least temporarily while you make changes to your life. Are you able to work from home one day or more a week? This could be helpful to address external practical factors or break up the interactions in a toxic workplace.

- Develop yourself. Speak to human resources and see if you can go on any courses to enhance assertiveness, time management or well-being, or see if you can have a mentor or coach. Use your time within your organisation to develop yourself. Go back to your original job description and see if you are still doing the things you were brought in to do in the first place, or if this has slipped and you need to realign them.

- Enhance your time out of work. Create time outside work doing things that give you energy and excitement, and which feed your true authentic self. (See the Social and Play action points.)

- Develop a side hustle. This is a part-time business or freelance work that you do in addition to your full-time work or alongside other part-time work to bring in additional income. Ideas include blogging or creating content, especially if you like writing or enjoy making informative videos which you could monetise on a YouTube channel. If you are an expert in a particular area or subject you could offer freelance services, online tutoring or courses to earn extra income.

  If you are crafty or are having a spring clean or clear out and have a knack for recycling or buying vintage or handmade items, then you could start a shop on an online marketplace to sell your wares. If you have a spare bedroom, you could list it as a vacation rental on a platform such as Airbnb for travellers or businesspeople who need accommodation for a short period. That way the bills still get paid and you have developed a new source of vitality and income in your life while still honouring your commitments.

  I have always found that if I had two streams of income it helped me to sleep better at night as I was never reliant on one stream to provide everything. I guess this is just my cautious nature coupled with the fact that I was a single parent for many years and solely responsible for paying bills, so felt better not having all my eggs in one basket.

- Take holiday entitlement and sick leave. Breaks from a job you feel trapped in are essential. Consider using your holiday entitlement differently. Rather than booking a fortnight off, book a Friday or Monday off for 10 weeks and have a long weekend. We all know how excited we feel with a bank holiday coming up – a four-day week – great, so recreate this for yourself. Likewise, if the chance to take a daily lunch hour is unrealistic, then take four 15-minute breaks, step outside, stretch your legs or sit quietly where you won't be disturbed and meditate and concentrate on your breathing to activate your PNS and relax.

- Take time out, or if you qualify for sick leave then take this time to realign yourself and get your head straight about how work is the money-maker, but outside work is where you get your fulfilment. Start to act and put plans into place before returning to work – even if this is researching opportunities for yourself.

If you enhance your time outside of work you can reframe your work and focus on the positives such as bill paying, mortgage payments and the comfort your home life gives you and what you can provide for yourself or your family. Remind yourself of the bigger picture.

CAREER DERAILMENT

Career derailment refers to unexpected and unwanted changes in the trajectory of your career, often as a result of being overlooked for an expected promotion or as a direct consequence of organisational restructuring, particularly in times of economic decline. If your identity is based mainly around the job or work that you do, career derailment or loss of interest in your career can be devastating and the trigger for a midlife crisis. It can feel like an enormous part of you has been crumpled up and thrown away. If this has happened to you, you might be inclined to jump ship and get a job at a competing organisation. However, I would encourage the following action points:

- Check your enthusiasm. Take the opportunity to consider whether you had enthusiasm for the promotion and if they were right not to give you the promotion. You might even ask for an explanation and see if part of not getting the promotion was attributed to your energy or attitude at work. If so, consider why your energy or attitude might have changed. Maybe you know the hours you'll need to put in when you get this promotion are going to take you away from any kind of social life and that just doesn't appeal to you. Perhaps deep down you are fed up working for other people and leaving your working life to their discretion. Maybe you've always wanted to study for a new career or finally take that college course you've been meaning to for all these years but never had the time and maybe this is now the time.

- Divert the time you saved elsewhere. People can more easily tolerate a dull career if they have other areas of their life that vitalise them. If your career gets derailed and you lose your job or promotion, then consider spending the hours you would have ploughed into the new role on another area of interest in your life for pure enjoyment and satisfaction to boost your energy. So, do some online courses and get some books out of the library, learn a new skill and have a bit of fun, just for you.

CAREER CHANGE

Many of us remain in careers we chose and studied for at a much younger age. We're invested, but not necessarily happy. During our life cycle our wants, needs and desires can change.

You are never too old to change your career, because the upheaval of changing careers often outweighs the personal compromise to your well-being of staying in a job which strips away your vitality every day. However, don't start trawling recruitment sites yes but take action to;

- Clarify uncertainty. Be clear about it is within your current job that doesn't work for you anymore. Go back to page 134 and see the first action point in the Work section.

- Know what's stopping you. Be clear about what is the biggest obstacle or attachment that is making it difficult to change career, so you can divert your focus to it.

- Know what you want. Clarify what you truly want from a career, and what is fundamentally driving the change. Is it more flexibility and freedom or reduced stress and workload or do you want to start working from home more or be in a more rural setting to avoid traffic jams or do you need the flexibility to pursue other interests or family commitments? Be clear about what aspects of a career you are passionate about, what interests you the most and your goals and this will help to narrow down future career options. Research different careers that align with your interest and goals to clarify exactly what each one entails.

- Clarify the good stuff. Knowing what you enjoy doing/learning/developing in work can help you to pinpoint what's currently missing from your role and what are essential elements you need for your next role.

- Know your skills. Mastery in the workplace can be a great motivator. Being or becoming an expert at a skill you use regularly can boost self-esteem, well-being and satisfaction.

- Collate new information and resources. Look into any new skills you might have to acquire for the career change you are considering, where you could achieve this and what the networking opportunities are locally and more widespread for you. This will help you to know what you will need to do to make this transition a reality and the time and effort which is required.

- Update your CV. By updating your CV and profile on any business websites you can highlight your existing skills, the aspects that you are retraining in and your future ambitions. It will also let other firms know you are available.

- Get support. It's always helpful to gain support from a business coach or mentor in the new area of work you are looking to move into. Is it possible that you could do any voluntary work at an organisation to see if it is a good fit for you or meet with their human resources department for a chat to get a feel for the culture of the company and how employees are treated?

- Make your next move meaningful. Ensure the career change you choose is meaningful for you at a personal level. What is meaningful will vary between individuals, but generally work that contributes to your life, the lives of others, your community, society or the greater good is experienced as meaningful. When work is meaningful it can feel like a reward in itself.

EARLY RETIREMENT OR VOLUNTARY REDUNDANCY

Early retirement or voluntary redundancy can often look like an easier option and people will tell you just how lucky you are to be out of the rat race. However, if you enter retirement or voluntary redundancy without the self-awareness of how you will be spending all the extra time you now have available in a meaningful way, you could struggle and experience it as a crisis.

Retirement can be tricky! It's surprising just how many people take antidepressants for the first time in their life during retirement. Often the ending of a career or the finishing of a meaningful job into a big, open, empty retirement space can create a big identity shake-up, as one client said to me 'I went from hero to zero overnight when I retired'.

Having a lot of unstructured time on your hands all of a sudden is a classic trigger for a crisis due to the absence of identity and meaningful work. The divorce rate often rises for couples during retirement so really consider how you will fill your time if your partner isn't retiring with you. Think about whether you care deeply for a particular cause or if you are mad about animals and would want to volunteer at the local dog rescue centre. Retirement is a major life transition itself, grossly underestimated, and finding an identity in retirement is challenging, particularly if work has been a big part. However, with the right preparation and planning, retirement can be a fulfilling period of your life. The same can be true of voluntary redundancy.

Action points:

- Plan in advance. Before you leave, consider what your days are going to be like when work isn't a factor. How will you fill your days, what kind of social interaction do you want, and how will you find purpose and meaning in this expanse of time? Where possible, create a plan and be ready for how you intend to spend your days. Follow the formula above for a career change and ensure that you find things that fulfil you and boost your self-esteem and are meaningful and worthwhile for you. If you do find the situation happens unexpectedly, take the time to sit down, begin to plan, and create some structure for how you would like to use your retirement time, in line with your goals and values.

- Experiment with new ideas. Before you leave work completely, experiment with new hobbies and social groups which will help stave off any loneliness when your redundancy begins or seek out a new career or job. (See action points in Social.)

FINANCES

If your financial situation is causing you unhappiness, here is some guidance to change that situation. The reality is, you can't always make immediate adjustments to the overall state of your finances, but you can begin to identify a less worrying financial position and work towards it. This, in turn, might reduce your stress levels and increase your sleep.

Clarify and assess your current financial situation. You will need to look at your current income, expenses and outstanding debts. It can be a bit scary to get a sense of your overall financial picture, but it is essential if you are going to shake things up a bit and identify areas where you could potentially cut costs and increase income. It can be easy to hide your head in the sand because of how scary this is, but it really won't help you find a way to a better financial future – the only way is to face it head-on and make sense of where you are at. You could consider these action points:

- Define what good looks like for you. A healthy financial situation looks different for different people, so don't be influenced by others. Everyone has varying ideas regarding amounts they feel comfortable with to cover unexpected events, what they might be actively saving for retirement and what their net worth needs should be.

- Get your debts in order. List everything and see if you can do anything to consolidate with zero finance options or consolidate with low-interest rates.

- Set some financial goals. Use SMART principles (Specific, Measurable, Achievable, Relevant and Time-bound) for your goals to keep you on track and focused. Be clear about what you are trying to achieve financially in the short and long term. Financial goals might include; debt reduction, saving for retirement, paying off the mortgage and reducing other debts, creating an emergency fund for increased peace of mind, and saving for further education or a college fund.
- Set a personal budget. This can help you to get hold of your finances, enabling you to get a clear overview of money coming into your household and the money going out. Budgeting at any time of life is important but can become even more so in midlife as you may reduce your working hours to accommodate a family or other responsibilities, a change in income, planning for retirement or juggling work alongside ill health issues. A personal budget can be an important financial tool to identify both fixed and variable expenses allowing you to allocate money and restrict money in a way that aligns with your priorities.

    To get started on your budget, you'll need to work out how much you spend on:
    - household expenses (mortgage, rent)
    - living costs (groceries, utilities)
    - childcare or elder care expenses
    - education (school or university fees, tuition, daycare, subscriptions)
    - debt payments and financial products (bank charges, credit card debt or interest)
    - medical care (doctors, dentists, private health insurance),
    - personal expenses (hair, clothing, gym, hobbies)
    - family and friends (gifts, birthdays, entertainment, special occasion costs)

- → travel (public transport costs, parking and car costs such as fuel, and servicing)
- → leisure (holidays, gym fees, meals out or other entertainment)
- → savings (retirement fund, emergency fund, money set aside for specific events such as holidays or weddings)

You can use pen and paper to complete your budget, or an app (there are many free financial resource websites on the internet), which can help you itemise expenditures. With a personal budget, you are less likely to be caught out by unexpected costs, you are less likely to be overdrawn or in debt, and you will be able to positively change your credit rating which over time will make you more likely to be accepted for loans. Budgeting will also enable you to track your spending and target areas where you recognise you might be overspending.

- Invest in yourself. Prioritise your education and consider retraining and obtaining new skills or training which would make you more desirable in the job market and open up new, better paid opportunities.

- Step up. To take back some control in a situation where you feel control is limited, consider living frugally to try to save some money. This could entail bulk cooking or upcycling furniture rather than buying new. There are some great groups on Facebook with lots of interesting and money-saving tips. Even if this doesn't create enough money for you to make big changes that you might like, like paying off all your debt or leaving your job, it could give you back a sense of control and choice so maybe you don't have to work that extra shift or do overtime in a job you dislike. This can put you back into the driving seat of your life, making a difficult situation a little more tolerable.

- Find your tribe. Find a community that shares your views and is also working to get better control of their finances and has a positive attitude toward saving for the future. This might be a Facebook group that relishes upcycling or batch cooks to save money. Choose to hang around with people who have similar financial values to you and support you to take care of your finances without encouraging excessive spending.

- Call in the experts. Consider seeking the help of a financial planner or coach who can offer specific advice for your individual needs.

- Stay positive. As finances can't be changed overnight it is important to stay positive while you start to turn things around. Do things that bring joy or relief from the mundane, but which cost very little. Spend time with positive people who are good company whatever you're doing. Spend more time doing things that enhance well-being but cost little or no money, such as meditation or keeping a gratitude journal. See the Play section for more ideas.

- Cut back. Give up alcohol and any other expenses that don't enhance your well-being. Focus on creating new habits rather than goals. Get up, make your bed, tidy up, eat healthily, walk and stretch. Get out in the world in free spaces such as parks; learn to meditate; take photos. Concentrate on your sleep and do all the things that induce good sleep. Working on your mental and physical health can make you feel great, help strengthen your resolve and does not have to cost anything.

PLAY

GEORGE BERNARD SHAW SAID, 'WE don't stop playing because we grow old; we grow old because we stop playing'.[36]

You would imagine that playing and being playful would be the most natural thing in the world, but it isn't. Without realising, many of us stopped playing somewhere between childhood and adulthood when life became fuller and other priorities and responsibilities took over. As kids, we are often naturally playful, but as we get older, we seem to lose this skill, even to the extent that we devalue it and deem it unnecessary. The result is that many midlifers don't know how to play, even though they may have the time and resources to do so. Often, they feel guilty about taking time out and feel they should be working rather than taking time to enjoy themselves.

Play is an important part of our lives and continued happiness. It enhances our mental health, our mood, and our enjoyment in life when we do things that are fun, silly, make us laugh, or bring joy to our souls. To give ourselves space for play (whatever that looks like) in midlife is an amazing gift we can give ourselves – so I ask, can you give yourself permission to play? (And if not, can you take some time to think about why not?)

Everybody's idea of play is different, one person's idea of play might be to read new scientific research (or is that just me?) another might be to sweat it out on an hour-long spin session at the gym. Some people might prefer to sit for hours watching films, while others might prefer to do charitable work or walk with the dog. There's something very pure about the pastimes we engaged in when we were younger. They tend to be less society-led, less expensive and more about being with a group of friends and being free. Decisions about what games to play were made often without influence – you can't fake having a good time. Our early lives can hold the secret to our natural enjoyment of how to play before our adult self-became conditioned and sensible.

Deciding what 'fun' is for you as you age isn't always that easy, but funnily enough, it is one of those rare occasions when replicating childhood passions or activities can be beneficial! So here are some action points:

- Remember your childhood. Make a list of things you used to do as a child just for fun. Then see how these childhood activities might transfer into grown-up activities. Playing video games as a child could turn into an adult's Dungeons and Dragons online group, tap dancing might turn into a salsa or swing class, and riding your bike could turn into getting a motorbike and joining a club for ride-outs.

- Use the internet as a resource. To see what 'fun' might mean for you, use the internet to search 'fun things to do as an adult' or 'bucket list ideas' and when a long list appears, follow your natural interest and the body's response and see which activities you click on for further information.

- Play for health reasons. Playful activity is not only good for the soul, but it releases endorphins in the bloodstream which can help us release stress, reduce symptoms of anxiety and depression, enhances brain function and help create a feeling of well-being. Having a laugh with friends, having sex, meditation, exercising, relaxing, getting a massage, and spending time outdoors in the sun are all ways of releasing endorphins. Endorphins are often known as the body's natural pain reliever or stress release.

- Use science to find out how to play. If you're not sure how to play use science and research to guide you and see what appeals. In his book *Play*,[37] Dr Stuart Brown describes five play archetypes which he found prevalent in adulthood through his many years of research in this area. See which one resonates with you:

- → Rough-and-tumble play helps develop our ability to regulate emotions and master physical and cognitive skills. The category consists of high-intensity sports and competitions such as tug-of-war, British bulldogs, dodgeball and scavenger hunts.

- → Ritual play consists of sports and activities with set rules and structures such as board games, puzzles and sports that bring people together for a common purpose. There are many online groups which offer this.

- → Imaginative play allows an adult to let their ideas and imagination run wild. This play consists of storytelling, acting, painting, writing and colouring and goes some way to explain the popularity of adult colouring books over the last few years. Look out for local community workshops.

- → Body play fulfils our spontaneous desire to defy gravity and includes sports such as riding roller coasters, surfing and snorkelling. If this is your thing, there are many groups and daredevil opportunities on the internet. Maybe you could learn to fly a plane in your spare time or start small at your local pool or on holiday with a snorkelling lesson.

- → Object play is any play which involves the manipulation of objects, allowing us to return to the play that was familiar to many of us in childhood, such as Lego and building blocks. There are many online communities and conventions throughout the world that support this form of play.

- Use your values. Think of those aspects of play that might appeal to you and consider how this would tie in with your values and the sort of people you would like to spend time with.

- Decide who to play with. If life is demanding enough, then choose to play in a relaxed environment rather than a competitive one and decide whether you want to play alone or in the company of others
- Allocate time. Each week or month dedicate time to try out a new activity. If you don't enjoy it, that's okay at least you know and can take that knowledge and try it in another way. You might find that you need a quieter environment, need more movement, need to be more intellectually stimulated, or need to be in dialogue with others. There are no wrong answers, just new learning as you discover which activities fit you and how you want to spend your free time. (See action points in Social.)

SOCIAL

People seek out other people at all stages of life for human connection and contact. In midlife, it's essential you have the right quality of contact if your social life is going to be rewarding for the second half of life.

While many of the action points in Play are relevant here, an enormous part of social life is mixing with others and creating new friendships to counteract feelings of isolation and loneliness and boost well-being.

People start to lose friends from around the age of 25, and particularly in midlife, a person's social network begins to shrink. Unlike when we are younger, a consolidation process commences in these middle years as people choose to spend time with family members and familiar people they feel emotionally attached to, rather than new people. This choice fosters a feeling of well-being and social embeddedness but, of course, this isn't possible if your best friends, family and oldest acquaintances no longer live nearby.

This isn't helpful for people who may be looking to expand their social life as part of dealing with bereavement or becoming a single parent. Your social world can also be changed by marital, family or relationship breakdown or separation, where existing friends or family members have picked a side, and it isn't yours. You might also find yourself in a new home and perhaps a new part of the country due to family or job changes, which means you have to start afresh to make friends and build connections. If this is the case, you're going to have to make a conscious effort to get out there and meet new people, because stumbling across new friends doesn't often happen by chance. People change over time and often our friends have been with us for years.

Some people come into your life for a reason and that may be to help, support or guide you because you may have knowingly or unknowingly expressed a need outwardly and when it's been fulfilled, they move on. Others come along to share a particular time of life with you and they may teach you something, I often see this with single parents and the friends they make. Finally, some friends stay forever and can adapt and grow into the friendship alongside you.

Try the following action points to revamp your social life.

REASSESS EXISTING FRIENDSHIPS

- Don't be afraid to cull. People think it's a poor reflection on their character if they change friends, but there is a world of difference between a person who can't hold on to friends and one who outgrows their friendships and acquires new friends due to life taking on a different direction and existing friends not understanding or supporting their changes. If your life is changing, for example, you've decided you're no longer going to put up with your job or your relationship, any new changes can unsettle existing friends, especially if you've always empathised with each other about how rubbish work was or how disappointing partners are, but unlike you, they aren't going to do anything about it. You are taking action and that changes things – maybe it wasn't the friendship they signed up for, you discover you have less in common now things have changed, or it feels shaming for them to acknowledge what they haven't changed.

- Check their qualities. Clarify qualities you want in a friend. Being a good friend entails offering trust, loyalty, empathy, encouragement, listening, allowing other friends to be themselves and being supportive in the good times and the bad. By being non-judgemental but truthful, you can provide each other with emotional support and reliability. Surround yourself with people who are pleased to see you and whose eyes light up when you walk into the room and are always ready to help celebrate your wins.

- Invest in each other. Some friends will support you no matter what and they are the ones to hang on to. Good friends will be invested in your change; others who are not invested in your personal growth may not be worthwhile friends and may be draining your energy reserves and might have to be culled.

EXPANDING CURRENT FRIENDSHIPS

Current friends are part of your life already so invest in them further by considering these action points:

- Take the initiative. Suggest meeting for a coffee more regularly, going for a walk, or trying out new restaurants as they open up in your area that way you can get away from the more formal structure of a class or a club and just hang out.

- Get into the right mind frame. Many people find it difficult to ask for help and support, but I always say, 'If you knew a good friend was lonely and they asked you out for a walk, would you go?' The answer is usually, 'Yes of course.' People like to help other people. I found that if you are a very independent person then it can be very fulfilling for a friend to feel they are helping you, as the chance to offer support doesn't come up that regularly because you rarely ask.

- Ask for support. Changing the tempo of your current friendships can feel awkward, like you're putting pressure on friends to meet you. Consider having a conversation with them to let them know you need support, and it would be really helpful if they could see you more regularly for the next few months, while you expand your friendship group in other areas. That way, everything is transparent, and if they agree to support you, you can relax a little.

- Don't be afraid to reach out. If you're uncomfortable ringing friends, then text so they have time to consider your invite to get together. Try and put a date in the text to meet rather than leave it open-ended – it also gives them the chance to suggest a better date which works for them.

- Get to know your friends' friends. When your friends are going out in a group you don't know, ask if you can go along, chances are you'll meet another friend within the group who has the same qualities as you.

- Reconnect with an old friend. They were your friend for a reason but maybe you just haven't seen them for a little while. They can only say no, but generally, life gets busy in midlife and old friendships can slip. It's just life. If you don't ask the question, you'll never know. A simple text like, 'Haven't seen you for ages, do you fancy catching up over coffee next week?' What's the worst that can happen?

MAKE NEW FRIENDS

With more of us working from home, there is even less possibility of new social interactions and opportunities to meet new people, so opportunities have to be created by you. Here are some action points to consider.

- Get a dog. This will force you to get out and about – but don't put your earphones in, be available to chat. If you go to the same area at the same time of day, you'll meet the same people and can start up a conversation – even if it is initially about your dog!

- Do some charitable work. Now that you have updated your values, choose a charity which reflects those values. When you volunteer you are more likely to meet people who share those values. For example, The Global Red Cross Network has values centred around compassion and inclusion and Save the Children values accountability and ambition. Do any of these resonate with you?

- Look online. Here you can search for local groups because then at least you'll know that any members will live close by. You'll have more chance of regularly seeing any friends you make in the group elsewhere, too, as they won't live too far away.

- Start a local group. Choose an interest that you love, that way you get to control who joins and the focus of the group.

- Start online. If you are an introvert or tend to shy away from groups, it can be a good idea to recalibrate your social life by starting online and then moving into in-person groups.

- Shift the focus off friendship. Join a group where friendship is not the focus, but people meet to discuss books, to dance or to create an object like pottery or a furniture upcycling workshop. It could give you something to focus on, which allows friendships to develop more naturally. This can be particularly useful if you are shy meeting new people initially. Social network platforms such as Meetup.com offer varied local social events for people to meet as friends. The emphasis here is not on dating, so that takes a lot of the pressure off, especially if you are already in a relationship. Meetups include groups where you can learn a new language, chat about books or philosophy, or try out new restaurants as part of a regular supper club. They are local, which means you'll be more likely to find people who live near you should you decide to meet up outside of the group.

- Be charitable. Commit to doing something for charity, such as a walk for your local hospice, which ideally has a few weeks training programme or practice walks to get all the walkers in shape, so you'll see the same faces a few times as you get fit.

- Be practical. If money is tight, arrange a picnic with friends and take your own food – it's the company that's important, not where or what you eat.

- Visit the library. Instead of buying books, head down to your local library and see if they have details of any interesting talks or workshops coming up. Look for details of local community groups that give talks of interest, such as U3A, or help out at a local community project.

- Use social media. Follow influencers and join Facebook groups for tips on confidence building and on making a change in your life. Learn a new skill by watching YouTube videos such as upcycling or calligraphy or photography or learning to write. These skills and abilities may enhance your ability to then go out, feel more confident and make friends.

PARENTING

It's difficult to make generalisations about the relationships between midlifers and their children, as these relationships can vary greatly depending on the individuals involved and their unique circumstances and also the ages of the children.

I've split this section into three parts due to different ages, experiences and expectations of Gen X parents (born 1965–1980) and their Gen Z children (born in the mid-1990s – 2010). Many midlifers will have grown-up children making their way in the world and living independently outside the family home, others will be recent empty nesters, while others will have children just entering secondary school or in their early teen years, which brings with it a whole set of challenges.

Overall, there have been significant changes in relationships between midlifers and their children over the last 30 years. For example, there is increased contact between the generations, particularly supportive contact from midlifers whose adult children have difficulties. There has been an increase in shows of affection between the generations and an increase in the number of midlifers and grown children cohabitating.[38] I will explore some more of the common challenges below.

If this area of your life needs improvement, it's important to be clear whether your unhappiness is related to specific issues, dynamics or conflicts with your child or related to external pressures that impact you or them.

ACTIONS TO IMPROVE YOUR RELATIONSHIP WITH YOUR ADULT CHILD

Generational societal norms, changing styles and expectations mean that people of different ages have different approaches to how they live their life and bring up their children. Different dilemmas and challenges may arise for midlifers whose children are now adults. Here are some useful action tips to try to smooth over differences which cause tension:

- Show respect. Respect the autonomy of the adult child as you might respect anyone else in their teens or early 20s. It can be tempting to continually view them as a child but treat them as an equal and give them a voice. Keep in mind this is an adjustment process as you adapt to being a parent of an adult child. You cannot parent them the same way as a young child, as this is a more independent, adult relationship. You will be learning to navigate a new relationship together.

- Set personal boundaries. It can be common for some midlifers to feel taken for granted or undervalued by their adult child, especially when they are very involved in their life and help them out a lot. Make sure you are not overstretching yourself and creating tension because you're exhausted. Pull back to more manageable levels and hand back responsibility to them where possible.

- Be open and communicative with your adult child – it can be really important. For advice on handling complex dynamics or restructuring a relationship with an adult child, see conflict resolution strategies in the Family section.

- Accept their life choices. Rather than trying to change them, try and see life through their eyes, especially if their choices are not damaging or threatening. Ultimately, it is important to remember that adult children do not have to seek your opinion on or permission for any of their choices. You may want to share your views as a parent, but unless your child is asking, it is not necessarily helpful, particularly if you hold an opposing view to your child.

- Know when to apologise. If you know you have overstepped, then apologise. I know this can be problematic for many parents who may never have apologised to their child, but this behaviour is typical of an authoritarian parenting style and not how adults interact. You need to let go of control and be a consultant in your child's life, not a CEO.

- Respect differences. If you simply cannot agree with some aspect of their life, discuss this in a calm, adult way, recognising and respecting differences. There might have to be some accommodation on both sides, but the aim is to maintain the relationship. Remember you don't have to agree with everything they do, they may not be asking for your opinion.

- Learn to be tolerant. In time your family may expand with new family members and with them, the potential for new conflicts and differences of opinion. Different families coming together have different expectations and different experiences of how people interact and levels of respect and tolerance. Be open to accommodating new members and try to connect with these new members. Though they may try your patience with their ideas, try to focus on the positives of the relationship, for example, how that person keeps your adult child happy. Points of tension can arise between midlifers and their adult children around being disappointed or struggling to develop good relationships with the partner their adult children choose and disagreements regarding their life choices. Show your love. Offer unconditional love because this is a joy for anyone to receive.

- Try and create time together just for the fun of it, outside of any jobs you do to help them out.

- Find some common ground. Yes, you are related but you are very different people. Find a connection as adults and not as their parents. Tread carefully around sensitive topics such as politics, religion and ideology differences of opinions as these often cause ruptures between midlifers and their adult children.

- Communicate openly and honestly. As midlifers, health issues and caring for parents can limit the time you spend with your adult child and your availability to be with them. Be sure to communicate openly and honestly with them, for what you would like from them and also what they would like from you so that resentment doesn't set in, and you can maintain a positive and supportive relationship, which can ride the wave of changes and challenges experienced within the family.

- Seek out a professional therapist and engage in family therapy if you need help finding a new communication style. Relationships with adult children can change as children become more independent and establish their own lives. There are a growing number of midlifers who are still involved in the mental health and well-being or financial stability of their adult children.

ACTIONS TO IMPROVE YOUR RELATIONSHIP WITH YOUR GEN Z CHILD

Some different dilemmas and challenges may arise for midlifers whose children are still young and continue to require some level of care. Here are some useful action tips to try to smooth over differences which cause tension.

- Manage your time together. Integrating screen time into time spent together and family events is a way of appreciating that digital interaction has become an integral part of your Gen Z child's life. Gen Z prefers a mix of communication techniques and while talking face-to-face is important, it may be more so for you.

- Recognise different communication styles. Gen Z like to communicate and stay in touch via digital devices like email or text and like social media platforms where their post disappears within a certain amount of time rather than permanent postings on platforms such as Facebook which is preferred by midlifers.

- Show your love. Offer unconditional love because this is a joy for anyone to receive.

- Don't overstep. Don't be too overly involved in your child's life. Gen X tend to be very hands-on parents, so check with your child that you're not overstepping.

- Be aware of mental health. Encourage your child to seek out mental health support if that is their wish. Gen Z tend to have a greater understanding and awareness of mental health issues than Gen X parents did at their age and are more likely to seek support.

- Model acceptable behaviour. Your child or teen is always watching what you do such as how you interact with others, how you cope with stress. Model behaviour you would like your child to adopt, especially being able to handle and regulate your own emotions, self-care and taking time away from screens to relax.

- Encourage social contact. Supporting teens to mix with their peers in person so all contact doesn't happen online will help their social skills. Encourage this activity in a safe environment when you can.

- Discussing identity issues. Contemporary parenting can entail being available to discuss gender identity, gender roles, issues such as divorce and remarriage and gay and lesbian parenting.

As a general approach, it can be useful for Gen X parents to be available to talk to their children about the changing landscape of the world. Go at their pace, don't judge, stay open-minded, find out as much as you can about your child's opinion and be respectful of how they might want to be addressed. Adopting aspects of this approach may help you to connect at a deeper level with your child.

- Communicate openly and honestly. As midlifers, health issues and caring for parents can limit the time you spend with your child and your availability to be with them. Be sure to communicate openly and honestly with them. Be clear about what you would like from them and also what they would like from you so that resentment doesn't set in. This will help maintain a positive and supportive relationship, which can ride the wave of changes and challenges experienced within the family.

- Seek out professional help. Engage in family therapy if you need help finding a workable communication style.

ACTIONS FOR EMPTY NESTERS

When a child leaves home, so too can a large part of your identity as your role as a parent reduces. Bringing up a child for many people will have been the greatest source of meaning and purpose in their life. Often this purpose is not readily replaceable when a child leaves and this can cause people to feel lost as such a large aspect of their identity has disappeared. You developed skills and invested energy and time which supported your child's transition to adulthood and now it's time to use all these resources to support yourself and your development in this next stage of life. You can:

- Access professional help. This gives you a chance to process your emotions if you experience your child's departure as a profound loss. You may experience a whole host of feelings such as low mood, grief or anger. By taking responsibility for your own emotions, you avoid your child feeling pressurised to help you and changing their plans to support you.

- Consider other life changes. Be mindful that an empty nest can often happen around the same time as other transitions in your life such as perimenopause, menopause or andropause. Age-related hormonal changes can affect emotions, so it is important to pay attention to what your body needs to cope with these changes and support your mental health.

- Avoid catastrophising the situation. Remember that this isn't the end of your parenting duties. Parenting can still be needed by your child, just because they have left home doesn't mean they no longer need you. There will be emotionally challenging times when you can offer support, help them out and stay connected.

- Agree contact. It can be a good idea to agree how you and your child will keep in contact with each other, and the frequency of that contact, before they leave. This could be a phone call twice a week and maybe a daily text exchange. That way you can feel you still have a connection.

- Reconnect with yourself. The main thing here is to let the child go and concentrate on their growth as well as develop and concentrate on your personal growth. It's your time to find out what kind of person you want to be now that your responsibilities as a parent have reduced.

- Reconnect with old friends, some of whom might be in a similar position. Look at the action points in Play and Social to begin to recalibrate your life differently.

SPIRITUALITY

L IFE CAN OFTEN BE A bit of a rollercoaster and many people see spirituality as a way of ironing out some of the bumps, a resilience strategy used to cope with challenging situations and a way of finding peace, hope and comfort. People turn to spirituality as a way of finding meaning in the world, and a sense that there is something greater than themselves in the world. Often the words religion and spirituality are used interchangeably but religion tends to follow rules and practices within a group context, whereas spirituality is a much more individual experience.

Being spiritually aware can mean different things to different people. For one person becoming spiritually aware might mean being able to notice and be consciously aware of the world around them, such as hearing the noise the leaves make on a shaking branch or the hum of the traffic as it passes outside your window. For others being spiritually aware will mean becoming far more conscious of human existence, the fragility of life, how we are interconnected to others and who they are at their core.

To become more spiritual, you can consider the following action points:

- Begin a daily mindful meditation practice. Meditation is the practice of allocating specific time during the day to intentionally spend time with your mind. This time is spent learning to focus attention and awareness towards an emotionally calm state which can be beneficial for well-being, reducing stress and quietening down the chatter in your head.

Mindfulness has become a very popular practice over the last decade as people reach for some connectedness and to find some peace, quiet and solitude in a busy world. Being mindful helps to centre you in the present moment enabling you to become aware of what you are sensing and feeling in a non-judgemental way and without the need for interpretation.

Mindfulness meditation combines the quality of mindfulness within the practice of meditation. There are many videos on the internet and free exercises to guide you.

- Know your values. Some mindfulness practices specifically concentrate on your core values. When your actions are aligned with your values, they can bring contentedness and a sense of meaning to day-to-day activities.

- Meditate the same way daily. Doing the same meditation to start off with will help you perfect your process. This check-in will help to keep you on track and towards spending more of your time and life doing the things that support your wellbeing. With practice, this will become easier and part of your spiritual practice to align your day with your inner core. Meditation usually follows this process:

  → Sit comfortably in a place that feels calm and where you won't be interrupted. Use a chair, sit on the floor or kneel – whichever feels the most comfortable for you and you can be stable.

  → Set a time limit. Make this only a few minutes to start with, so you don't feel under pressure, and gradually build up time.

  → Slowly scan your body with your mind and notice each part of your body and how it is feeling. Try and connect with your physical self and be aware of all the physical contact your body is making such as with the floor or chair.

- → Focus on your breathing. Notice your breath, the rise and fall of your chest, and how your body responds.

- → Notice what is happening in your mind, what thoughts are coming and going? Just observe and notice them as they come and go. Notice when your mind flits to daily chores or something else and gently bring yourself back to this moment, and your mindfulness practice. Don't be cross if your mind gets distracted – this happens, just be kind and self-compassionate.

- → Close with kindness by repeating three positive reassuring phrases to yourself such as 'may I be safe', 'may I be strong and healthy', and 'may I be grateful for all that I have'.

• Cultivate self-awareness. Use your practice to become more self-aware, enabling your decisions to be made in line with your life plans and values.

• Plan your time. Consider what you are planning to do each day. Think about how you will spend your time and with whom, and if this feels like you are spending your time purposefully. Which values do these actions support?

• Reflect regularly. Taking the time to reflect on decisions and behaviour can reduce stress, keep us on track and reduce brain chatter and inner criticism. If actions are connected to values, you will know you are following the right path for you, which will reduce uncertainty.

• Practise self-care and self-love. When you practise self-care, you take care of yourself emotionally and physically. When you practise self-love, you are about cultivating self-acceptance and loving yourself unapologetically. You can begin to love and like yourself and accept your flaws and the things you might not do so well or would prefer to do better. It can boost self-esteem, without having to rely on anyone or anything else to do so and lead to greater personal happiness, forgiving yourself for any minor mishaps.

- Celebrate the small things. In practice, this might be to celebrate the small things you do in life, and how you have been with others and acknowledge your kindness, and good qualities via the form of a compliment.

- Listen to your body. Self-care is about looking after your body and meeting your needs. Exercise, eat well and sleep well. Give your body the fuel and nourishment it needs in the right amounts. A balanced self-care routine would include supporting yourself mentally, physically, emotionally, and spiritually. Think about the idea of taking care of yourself in a way that feeds your soul and brings you joy, you can see how this connects with what is important to you deep in your soul at a spiritual level.

- Connect with others on a deeper level. Develop friendships that are supportive as you continue on your journey. Spend time with those who are dear to you as feeling close and connected to people can be warming for the soul. Be a good friend and companion by listening actively to others and being able to give and receive feedback and criticism to ensure an authentic connection develops where you feel cared for and loved by the other. Stay open and non-judgemental and empathic.

- Keep a gratitude journal. This is a way of keeping a note of things that have happened to you or that are meaningful to you so that you can record, remember and reflect on the things that you are grateful for regularly. Often, when we feel quite low, it is easy to think that there's nothing good going on in your life or recall anything that ever felt good. When you have a journal, and you complete it you have information and entries to look back on. The process of keeping a journal can be as follows:

- Chose a journal or notebook you like the look of.
- Decide on the number of entries you will write down that you're grateful for each day.
- Set aside time for writing, it may only need to be five minutes.
- Start small if you need to, such as having a bed to sleep in, electricity to heat the house, and food in the cupboard.
- Make notes on a good day as you will be able to reflect on these entries as evidence of just how grateful you can be to support you on a day when things are tough. Journal entries can be motivational and a perfect reminder that every day is not a bad day.

FAMILY

MIDLIFE ADULTS ARE OFTEN KNOWN as the 'pivot' generation as they offer support to generations of their family above (parents) and below (children). For many midlifers, family is often one of the most important aspects of life. As people reach midlife there can be increasing contact with family members as parents become older, grandchildren come along, or time is spent supporting your adult children to find their way in the world.

In this section, I offer actions to improve and resolve family conflict, whatever the nature of the disagreement, and then consider actions to improve issues arising from caring responsibilities. It is recommended that therapy support, either individual or family/couple support, can be helpful if there are significant challenges or changes in family relationships that are difficult to resolve and are affecting your health.

Causes of unhappiness within families can include:

- inheritance issues
- conflicting values and lifestyles
- how people spend their money
- how they live their life
- personality differences
- unresolved previous conflicts and family issues
- overstepping of personal boundaries or control issues

- differing expectations
- poor communication and past issues
- time constraints due to caring responsibilities
- adjustments to major life changes such as a change in family structure or a new baby

While all these areas are not addressed individually here, this section offers midlifers action points on how to resolve family conflicts and how to cope with pressures arising from taking on care responsibilities, whether for elderly parents, grandchildren or partners.

CONFLICT RESOLUTION

As noted above, there are many reasons why family conflicts can arise, especially into adulthood when there are so many areas that can potentially result in differences of opinion or unhappiness/conflict. The shift in roles can play a big part in this, such as midlifers becoming carers for elderly parents; elderly parents being cared for by their children; midlifers learning to navigate new adult relationships with their independent children and with the new partners of their adult children; and learning to be grandparents.

When conflict arises, conflict resolution strategies can be helpful as a way of trying to open dialogues around issues, whatever the cause. The aim is to either find an agreed middle path that will work toward an attainable goal, or to decide not to engage further as contact has been futile. The following actions will help:

- Clarify the issue. Before jumping in to try and solve the conflict, focus on making sure you understand what the conflict or issue is about. You can gather information and seek input from others, which might help you identify the root cause of the issue if the current issue has changed from the original issue, and what approaches have been successful/unsuccessful in the past to address or resolve the issue. When you feel you have all the information you need, summarise the issue for yourself so you have a clear understanding of it before you go ahead and discuss or negotiate the issue with another party.

- Negotiate. This is a process of communication between two parties whereby issues are discussed to find a mutually acceptable solution. Having clarified the nature of the issue, begin the negotiating process in a neutral location and within a positive atmosphere. Setting ground rules can be helpful such as respecting each other's differences, setting time limits for discussion, contracting to keep conversations confidential and agreeing to stay calm and kind towards one another. Not all issues can be resolved and so will need a different approach, see below.

- Spot unresolvable issues. Sometimes it's impossible to reach an agreement or settlement despite your best efforts. These perpetual problems need managing because they can't be solved. They can occur as a result of people's differences in needs or opinions, how you relate to each other, personality differences, lifestyle preferences, family duties and differing expectations and goals. The ideal position to reach is an acceptance and understanding of the other's position (this does not apply to abusive or toxic behaviour which is unacceptable). If you decide to try and talk about this unresolvable issue it can be useful to agree to disagree and use accommodation as a strategy as, even though this doesn't close the gap between the differences, it can help both parties to take a step closer to one another. A smaller gap between differences can be much easier to manage than a standoff position.

- Accommodate when necessary. This a useful strategy in a situation between parties who have a strong relationship. An ideal outcome of accommodation is that a middle ground is found where each party is willing and motivated to give up something to resolve the conflict. This strategy can be helpful to preserve relationships, but it is really important that you don't compromise yourself, your values or your morals too much by agreeing to something that you don't think is fair or reasonable or that sits uncomfortably with you. It can help if both parties are willing to compromise and make concessions to reach an agreement that meets everyone's needs. Once an agreement has been reached ensure that you carry out any commitments made during the negotiation in the time allotted to ensure a positive relationship continues with trust should the need to negotiate arise again in the future.

- Avoid if you must. This involves steering clear of the issue and not discussing it at all, which can be okay if the problem is only of minor interest or value to you or if addressing the problem would open up a far more toxic can of worms and do more harm than good. Generally, it is not ideal to completely avoid issues as often they can turn into bigger issues and rarely do problems go away on their own.

- Set boundaries. This can be useful in conflict resolution to agree on ground rules for the process between one party and another so family members (such as overbearing in-laws) know the behaviour that will not be tolerated. It can keep the discussion on track and create a sense of safety for you and the other parties involved, which can encourage people to communicate honestly and openly.

- Know when to be transparent. It can be helpful to be authentic in interactions with family members, but you don't necessarily have to share all your thoughts and feelings with them, just those that might be relevant to reduce conflict or bring an end to outstanding issues. For example, if you are unable to offer money towards a shared expense for an elderly relative it might be helpful to let your siblings know why this might be to avoid them thinking that you are disinterested or do not care.

- Manage stress. In tense situations such as family arguments, it can be of the utmost importance to manage your stress levels. All adults are responsible for regulating themselves emotionally and it is important to remain in control of your emotions when dealing with an issue with another party. Being aware of the other party's emotions and suggesting a time out if the situation is becoming unstable or elevated can be useful to help reset the situation until both parties are more in control and can return to prioritising the need to reach a resolution.

- Identify useful conversations. Use a blueprint for how to communicate in the future if further issues arise. This blueprint can then be used to avoid wasting time on interactions which are not productive or informative. A useful conversation is a productive, informative and positive conversation between parties which leads to a better understanding of an issue or moves parties towards a resolution. Useful conversations allow relationships to be strengthened, trust to grow, and helpful and informative views and ideas to be exchanged. Knowing when to exit heated unproductive conversations that do not have the elements required for a conversation to be useful can also be helpful.

- Access mediation. This is a process which involves a neutral third party (the mediator) helping to facilitate communication between parties when they have been unable to reach a mutually acceptable agreement. The mediator helps resolve conflicts in a non-adversarial way and can be useful for financial matters or matters relating to the care of elderly parents between siblings. Mediation can provide a safe, neutral and non-judgemental space for family members to discuss concerns, be heard and be encouraged to come to a solution which meets everyone's needs.

- Cut ties. When negotiation feels futile due to dysfunctional family relations and despite your best efforts to resolve any conflict, you may need to consider cutting ties with certain family members. Before making a big decision like this it is necessary to consider realistically whether the other party has the potential for change, understands and acknowledges the issue at hand, and is motivated to work towards a healthy, mutually acceptable solution. Some people (such as those with manipulative or narcissistic personality traits) may not see a need to change and their lack of empathy, refusal to accept any criticism, and inflated sense of self hinder any meaningful progress. Remember this cut doesn't have to be forever. People can change over time and if you see evidence that the other party is regretful, more understanding of your position and truly wants to restart the relationship and make amends then you can consider engaging in a process of reconciliation.

CARE RESPONSIBILITIES FOR ELDERLY PARENTS AND/OR GRANDCHILDREN

The extent to which the middle generation has to take responsibility for the care of elderly parents and/or grandchildren differs between families. Some midlifers may never have to engage with this as other people or siblings assume this role, while some midlifers have to reduce working hours and rejig their life to support and accommodate family members.

Caring for ageing parents

Increased life expectancy in the last hundred years means there is more contact than ever between midlifers and their ageing parents. As both midlifers and their ageing parents live longer it is expected that an increasing number of midlifers will become involved with caring for their parents while working full-time and dealing with the health issues that accompany midlife. It Is estimated that in the UK and USA, approximately one in every five adults is currently providing care to an adult with health or functioning needs, and a significant percentage of those carers will be in midlife.

Caregiver activities for older family members can involve household tasks, such as food shopping, and preparing meals, emotional and social support such as companionship, health and medical care such as managing and giving medication and encouraging self-care, advocacy duties such as arranging doctor and social care appointments, and mobility and supervision duties such as bathing, dressing, and feeding.

A caregiving role can be highly variable. For some, it will follow a trajectory of increasing care responsibilities over time such as when a relative becomes increasingly unwell or caring for someone with dementia where there is a progressive decline in cognition and functionality over time. For some situations such as for stroke caregivers, the trajectory can begin with sudden intensity and gradually become less intense as the relative gains back some of their skills and the need for caregiving stabilises and reduces. For carers looking after relatives with cancer, caregivers may have to quickly take on the role as clinical decisions are made regarding treatment, and treatment commences.

In general, it is considered a positive experience to be a grandparent. Yet striking the right balance between giving of your time, responsibility and fulfilment and finding a sense of purpose and meaning in providing this can be challenging.

Grandparenting

Grandparenting can involve challenges such as having to change your natural parenting style to comply with your adult child and their spouse and their wishes for how their children should be looked after. There may be differences in expectations about how much grandparents will be involved with the children. If there are any relationship problems between your adult child and the spouse, you may end up providing emotional support for the children or having the children more because of unstable home life.

Being a grandparent can also be hugely rewarding and enjoyable and can help reduce stress and financial burdens for your adult children which might make a difference to their quality of life, especially if they are struggling to cover childcare, finding parenting overwhelming, divorced, or have increased responsibility and bills to pay, or night work away often or long shifts to work.

If grandparenting becomes full-time, for example, if a grandparent takes on full custody of a grandchild, extra personal care and attention are required because stressors can include financial strain, insufficient social support, lifestyle disruption, and being disregarded by service providers.[39]

The amount of time and responsibility midlifers are involved with their grandchildren varies tremendously between families. Some will provide occasional babysitting while others do the school run and spend a large amount of time in a custodial role for their children. If you can balance the right amount of intensity and frequency for you, then research shows it can be beneficial for an individual's (midlifer) cognitive functioning, quality of life, physical health and longevity.[40] If your caring is detrimental to your health, then step away from this role or reduce your contact and concentrate on your well-being.

Action points if caregiving is a cause of dissatisfaction in your life

- Strengthen your mental and physical health. Take a look at the action points in Relaxation and Health to help strengthen your mental and physical health and to give your body some downtime, even if time is limited. It is so important to get the balance right between your caring responsibilities and your self-care.

- Access help. If you are struggling with an aspect of your caring role, consider seeking help and support from other family members, friends or a therapist. It is important to have your network of support. Don't assume they know you need help, ask them for it.

- Use conflict resolution. If there are caring arrangements in place which just are not working for you then using the conflict resolution strategies above can be helpful to begin to renegotiate them to a regime which works better for you.

- Get organised. If you are feeling overwhelmed with your caring role, then get organised. This can help you feel more in control of a situation which is often out of anyone's control. Keeping a planner can help you prioritise tasks and a large folder can help you keep all your paperwork in one place. Keeping a notebook can be handy to write down observations for any future medical assessment meetings, and a large wall calendar to write appointments on can be a great backup and reminder alongside entries you might make on a mobile phone app.

- Focus on the positive. Focusing on positive aspects of caregiving can help mitigate the negative effects of it, such as a sense of burden and depression. Many people find caregiving rewarding and the positive psychological effects of this work include an appreciation of life, personal growth, closer relationships and self-efficacy and the way you feel about how well you are performing. Doing something well can enhance a sense of mastery and this can fuel a sense of purpose and meaning in your life.

- Find your tribe. Counteract loneliness with online support groups and carers' associations meetups and groups, as juggling caregiving alongside work commitments can be very challenging and can lead to a sense of isolation.

- Don't neglect yourself. Keep your energy charged by doing things you love to do. (See action points in Play.) If you are happy, you have more capacity and can give more to others.

Everyone benefits when you make time for yourself and have some fun. Ensure you are balancing the other areas of your life so that you are resting and still socialising and accessing support. If any of your caregiving is voluntary and it is making you unhappy and having a detrimental effect on your health and well-being, then step back from this role and concentrate on yourself if it is harming you.

- Access financial support. Look into any carer benefits you are entitled to and access them.
- Contact a therapist. Consider professional help if you are saddened by the change in the dynamic of your relationship with the person you have become a carer for. Don't suppress feelings, as this can use up valuable energy, but find a safe, supportive outlet such as a private therapist or support group to express and process them.
- Prioritise communication. To manage your role as a grandparent, communication with your adult child and their family is of the utmost importance here to establish boundaries and the nature of the care.
- Keep life as balanced as possible. A knock-on effect of taking on care responsibilities is that midlifers' sleep, work, relationships and family time can be adversely impacted, along with their retirement income (due to reduced hours in work, taking a less demanding lower paid job or having to take early retirement), future employment prospects, and their health and well-being. If you are becoming worn out with caring, looking after yourself is crucial. Caring can be emotionally and physically demanding and it's so important to keep your life in balance if you want to stay well enough yourself to continue your caring responsibilities. For any carer, the most important person to care about is you because more often than not, as I say to clients, 'If you go down, the whole ship goes down.'

HEALTH

As we get older our health becomes more important. Doing everything you can to stay well physiologically and psychologically in midlife is essential for overall peace of mind and well-being. Here I will concentrate on action points to improve mental health followed by action points to improve physical health.

MENTAL HEALTH

Rates of depression and anxiety are highest in midlife[41] so it can be important to manage your mental health well. If you feel you need support to understand and work through your feelings and thought processes, then contact a professional therapist who will work with you towards a solution. Depression, anxiety and other mental health challenges can adversely impact the quality of home life, create difficulties in your work life and impact social activities. Here are some action points to consider:

- Connect with people. This will help to give you a sense of belonging and enjoyment, and provide you with emotional support. In return it can also support other people to share life experiences with them. We know that social connection has been shown to enhance our mood and well-being. (See action points in Social.)

- Increase your physical activity. Regular exercise is good for the mind because it releases chemicals called endorphins. These are the body's natural painkillers that activate opioid receptors in the brain, helping to reduce pain and discomfort as well as triggering feelings of euphoria and well-being. Even a daily walk is effective. Find an activity that you love that enables you to move your body and do more of this.

- Get medical clearance. Always get the okay from your doctor before starting a new exercise regime. Ask for advice on specific exercises if you have conditions such as osteoporosis, high blood pressure or arthritis. An exercise routine for all-around well-being would concentrate on cardiovascular fitness, strength and improving balance and flexibility. It can increase self-esteem and confidence, relieve stress and benefit your overall mood.

- Eat well. Reflect on your food choices and explore ways to eat a healthy balance of all foods.

- Learn something new. Learning a new skill gets those brain neurons firing up, it can be good for feelings of achievement, self-worth, enjoyment and more.

- Work on your self-esteem. Creating a positive sense of how you feel about yourself can really enhance the quality of your life. (See action points in Self-esteem.)

- Chose meaningful activities. By engaging in activities that are meaningful for you, you can increase your sense of achievement and enjoyment. Do fewer of those activities that drain you and make you feel miserable.

- Be brave. Face your fears and reduce avoidance in any area of life where you recognise tackling issues and creating new ways of living would benefit you. Focus on living the life you want.

- Don't be a mind reader. Don't try and control what people think of you. Everyone will give their opinion on whether you're doing things right or wrong, all you need to be sure about is your path forward. Rather than waste energy trying to convince others, spend that energy on yourself and concentrate on the things in life that you can change.

- Relax. Use relaxation and mindfulness exercises to reduce stress and help ground you in the present moment. (See action points in Relaxation.)

- Sleep well. Focus on getting a good night's sleep. Sleep hygiene is a set of behavioural and environmental recommendations designed to help you get a night of decent quality sleep, such as controlling the temperature of your bedroom, stopping caffeine and alcohol for at least four hours before you go to bed, and getting up after 20 mins of trying to sleep if you are still awake. There are plenty of free resources on the internet to support you in implementing sleep hygiene conditions. Improving the quality and length of your sleep can be enormously beneficial for the mind and body giving both a chance to recharge.

- Engage with a therapist. See a therapist to work through any issues you are finding difficult to resolve. Join a local support group which specialises in supporting people to address a particular challenge in their life such as overcoming a divorce, reducing alcohol intake, dealing with anxiety or becoming a carer. These groups can help normalise your situation and offer an accepting environment with others experiencing similar life situations to you. Explore if medication would be right for you if needed.

- Chose good friends. Maintain supportive friendships and choose who you spend your time with. Ensure it is people who have your well-being at heart and support your personal growth and the changes you are actively making. Get support around you from people who understand your need to change or who love you and want to be there for you (see Social action points).

- Respect your values. Move forward making decisions based on your current values, not on other people's expectations of you or what they think would be best for you. Live according to what you truly want for yourself. Make sure that the decisions in your everyday life support your current values and needs and your authentic self and who you are striving to be.

PHYSICAL HEALTH

Over a third of adults in midlife have multiple health problems[42] and disability rates for midlifers are increasing too.[43] Potential explanations include rising rates of obesity, increased calorie intake and reliance on processed foods accompanied by low physical activity rates.[44]

Research shows that being overweight or obese in midlife increases the risk of dementia, vascular dementia and Alzheimer's disease in later life[45] and is a strong cancer risk factor. Being overweight also increases the risk of high blood pressure, coronary heart disease, stroke, and generally all causes of death.

The amount of muscle in our bodies decreases with age. This generally leads to lower metabolism, which makes it harder to keep excess weight off unless you control what you eat.[46] The World Health Organization and the Centre for Disease Control and Prevention recommend 30 minutes of exercise a day, five to seven days a week.

When compared to young adults and people of older age, middle-aged adults across affluent nations report more sleep problems, severe headaches and alcohol dependency.[47]

Living with health issues, pain or illness can be very challenging, but here are some actions you can take to improve the quality of your physical health:

- Follow advice. Take care to follow any medical and health professional advice you receive about taking care of yourself, daily rehab exercises or medication regimes.

Take regular exercise. It is never too late to start working out and it can help improve joint and bone health, lower risk factors for cardiometabolic disease and fight against age-related muscle loss. It also improves mental health and cognitive functioning. Maintaining functional independence can help improve the quality of your life. Seek advice from a medical professional if you are unsure about your abilities or how to get started.

Regular exercise can help chronic pain by strengthening and building muscle to support your body and improve function and has many mental health benefits, including improving the quality of your sleep. (See action points on sleep in Mental Health.) Too little sleep has been related to cardiovascular issues. Try and keep active throughout the day rather than in short energetic bursts, this puts less pressure on your joints.

- Keep your body supple. Take up yoga to help with joint flexibility and improve cardio and circulatory health.

- Eat healthily. This would include reducing processed foods and meats, alcohol and soft drinks. Increase proteins such as in poultry, lean meats, tofu, fish and eggs and whole grains such as brown rice, oats. Increase fresh or frozen fruit and vegetables and healthy fats, such as nuts and avocados.

- Check out local fitness groups held in parks if you don't want to exercise alone. Some people prefer a group activity for motivation and the social element, so check out your local gym, parks or dance classes.

- Work out. Doing this at home can be useful if you feel self-conscious or get distracted by other people. You could buy some dumbbells and begin to work out at home. There are lots of brilliant online dance classes, fitness apps or workout videos you can follow if you choose to do this from the comfort of your own home.

- Start walking. There is no expensive outlay for this, and you don't need any equipment other than a good pair of supportive shoes or trainers. Walking is a cardiovascular exercise, which strengthens the heart and burns calories.
- Try different pain management techniques. Experiment and find a way to help manage your pain such as physical therapy, massage, or acupuncture. Different treatments work for different people.
- Tackle the effects of chronic illness. Regular gentle exercise can improve symptoms and a sense of well-being, and the above exercises can be incorporated into your life. If you're in any doubt check with your doctor first.
- Manage your pain. There is an increasing body of evidence which suggests that using CBT can help people manage their chronic pain. CBT can focus on stress reduction and pain management techniques by identifying situations that trigger elevated levels of stress and the thoughts you have related to the situation. Working with a CBT therapist can help you to restructure your thoughts around these situations into more helpful ones, which can also trigger the PSN to reduce stress and aid relaxation.
- Manage hormone fluctuations. With midlife comes reduced hormones. Speak to your doctor for advice on the best way for you to manage reduced hormone levels.

RELATIONSHIPS

When relationships are going well, the world can seem like a better place. Love, however, isn't always easy and over the course of a relationship, as people change, their feelings for one another can change too. It is normal in a relationship that you will face periods of challenge or feeling unsure about wanting to be with your partner. People change and develop and grow at different times during a relationship. How these changes are tackled and worked through can be the deciding factor in whether couples stay together.

Here I offer action points and questions to reflect on regarding challenges for couples, individuals, being single and dating.

WORKING OUT WHAT IS GOING WRONG IN YOUR RELATIONSHIP

There are many reasons why relationships can be unhappy or under strain. A lack of intimacy, betrayal, trust issues, poor communication, neither of you is trying to better the relationship, you might have resolved to stay together despite unhappiness, or you may be waiting for some other event to take place before you leave (the house selling, the children leaving, finances being sufficient, refusal to divorce). However, living in an unhappy relationship can be debilitating emotionally.

Just like a car needs maintenance over the course of its lifetime to keep it running smoothly and repair any faults, so too does any relationship. The most important thing is to work out what is happening for you and where the relationships might be going wrong. Take action or begin by answering the questions below to help clarify this.

- Work out what needs to change. If you woke up tomorrow and your partner's behaviour towards you was perfect, what would they be doing differently? What would they be saying and how would the two of you be interacting? How would this affect how you reacted and behaved with them?

- Write an 'ideal partner' list. Whether you've been with your partner twenty years or twenty months, how clear are you about what you are looking for in a partner? How well does your partner fit this list? Do you still like and respect each other? Do you want to spend time with your current partner?

- Don't compromise yourself. Go back to the values and needs you identified in Exercise 2: Recognising my values (page 26) and assess how present they are within your relationship with your partner. Which needs are being met and which are absent? If you value success and popularity and your partner is an introvert with little ambition who wants to stay in, then unless there are enormous changes on your part or your partner's then it's unlikely these values will be met.

- Take the initiative. Are you waiting for your partner to change before you do? This can become frustrating and another issue within the relationship. Why not set some ground rules for how you communicate and interact together? This may help the contact between the two of you and lead to a positive shift within the relationship.

- Work out what you want to do together. Do you want to spend more time together, or apart? Do you want to travel, dine out more often, have more adventures? Think about the lifestyle you want and how near or far away from living that lifestyle you currently are. Consider what are the limiting factors holding you both back from living this way.

- Are you still in love? Are you comfortable in your relationship but no longer in love with your partner? Are you living separate lives with the relationship? Is this okay for you because comfort and security are your greatest needs and more important than excitement or romance?

- Are you intimate together? Consider how affectionate and intimate you and your partner are, how often you have sex, and how often you snuggle up together. Is this enough for you? Do you want something more regularly or do you not want it at all, yet your partner does? How often do the two of you communicate what you want and need to each other?

- How do you feel? It's important that you are clear how you want to feel in a relationship. Do you want to feel valued, respected, prioritised, trusted? If you currently don't feel these things, then work out when they might have stopped and what factors contributed.

- Are you attracted to your partner? How often do you tell them? Has either of you let your physical appearance go? Does this bother you? How attractive do you think you are to them?

- How is your communication? Do you regularly check in with each other? It can be helpful to set aside time each week to sit down, communicate and catch up.

- What makes you smile? What are the areas of your relationship that work well, make you smile and bring you joy?

- How much do you love yourself? How much of a catch do you think you are? How proud of yourself are you? How is your own self-esteem? If it is low, how do you think this impacts how you are in your relationship?

- How is your mental and physical health? Are you taking care of your own well-being and if not, why is that? If you feel well within yourself, this can support you through challenging times in your relationship.

- Do you have anaesthetising behaviours? Are you drinking too much, overeating, or taking drugs? How available are you to engage fully with yourself and your partner?
- Is there anything you are putting off? Are you avoiding a conversation because of the potential outcome, a career change, or maybe a lifestyle change? How is this delay affecting your energy and zest for life in your relationship?
- Is abuse present in your relationship? Is there emotional, sexual or physical abuse or manipulation taking place within your relationship? Are you being treated cruelly or disrespectfully by your partner? Are you safe?
- What are your disagreements about? Are they along the same theme over and over or do new issues arise frequently in your relationship? How do you manage these disagreements? Are they resolved?
- Respect each other. How respectful to each other are you regarding boundaries? Do either of you overstep boundaries regularly?
- How bored are you in your relationship? What do you put this down to? How often do you or your partner suggest doing new activities together?
- Is betrayal a factor? Have you experienced betrayal and has the trust disappeared from your relationship and you're unsure how to trust again? Do you think you're being lied to?

DECIDING TO STAY OR GO

If you are still unclear despite answering the questions above, it would be worthwhile contacting a professional therapist to help you both unravel and clarify issues and help you work towards solving them if that is what you choose to do.

Knowing whether to stay or leave a relationship can be complicated. Consider the following questions and actions:

- Create a list. Weight up carefully the reasons for staying and the reasons for going. Use facts, both positive and negative, to create a list. You might intuitively know the answer to whether you want to stay or go, or you might have accessed the wise figure within to lead you to your answer, but still, it is essential that you understand and name clearly the reasons for your actions and the history behind those actions. Create this list either on your own or in a non-judgemental environment such as with a therapist. Friends and family might have their own agenda and try to sway you one way or another.

- Are you being abused? Abuse is a clear reason to leave a relationship. There can never be any justification for someone abusing another person. How to leave safely is the most pressing decision. Work out what or whose support you need to leave.

- Rate your happiness. Does your relationship enhance your life or detract from it? What value does your relationship add to your life, does it make you feel happier, invincible, and understood?

- Consider what you'd miss. If you were to leave your partner and the life behind you, what are the factors you would miss the most and can you replace these elsewhere?

- Manage your expectations. Are the expectations of your relationship and partner realistic? Do you expect your partner to make life more interesting for you, be there for your every need, and make up for your shortfalls? I recommend the book *The Eden Project: in search of the magical other* by James Hollis[48] to clarify the reality of your expectations.

- Check your commitment level. If you know you have issues within your relationship, are you prepared, motivated and committed to working towards change and is your partner committed to doing so too? Both parties need to be motivated to work at reviving the relationship. Often one partner will be more motivated and invested in the relationship than the other, but both need to be willing to try for a relationship to be saved. A relationship takes two people so both of you will need to take an honest look at your current situation. Both must take responsibility and be willing to change how they contribute towards worsening the situation and what they need to do, act and say to improve the relationship. Are you both committed to doing this?

- Is fear keeping you trapped? Do you want to leave your relationship, but feel too scared? Work out the nature of the fear: is it fear of making the final decision, fear of being alone, fear of the unknown, fear of judgement, is it being able to afford your lifestyle on your own, or your own limiting beliefs? People who feel trapped can often make poor choices. Check if your fear is perceived or very real. Seek out professional support to help you work through these barriers so you can make an informed decision about whether to stay or go, without fear swaying you either way.

- Can you take criticism? Are you both prepared to be advised by the other if you are slipping back into old habits which threaten the success of the relationship continuing? Can you take constructive criticism from your partner, and can they take it from you?

- Find support. Do you have the social support you need if you leave and the finances to cover an increase in bills and the practical resources to get the children to and from school?

- Are you on the same page? Values, needs and goals change throughout life and for a relationship to survive, both parties need to be motivated to work together towards finding mutual values, and goals and exploring and achieving what each other needs. It is important to keep respectful and honour each other's differences, is this possible?

- Are you both growing? Change happens in life: people change, both due to circumstances and life experiences. Are you invested in each other's personal growth as human beings? Can you agree to hear each other's plans and goals without judgement? Do you want to turn towards your partner rather than away from them because you are both on the same team, navigating the world?

- What stops you leaving? Answer this: 'if you knew that if you left, you would be okay emotionally and financially, would you go?'

- Do you need professional support? It is natural to feel hurt and angry if someone you love and trust has been unfaithful to you. It is important to work out what you want to do from now on. It is essential to fully process your emotions and understand why this has happened, and to begin to heal yourself and repair your emotions before you decide to stay or go. It can be helpful to talk through your options with a therapist in a safe, non-judgemental environment so you can fully explore your feelings. When trust has been broken you can easily become suspicious, hypervigilant and a bit obsessive about a partner's behaviour and whereabouts. Talking this through with a therapist can allow you to stop any negative self-talk and regain trust.

- Make your decision. Make your final decision when you feel balanced, and calm and are not emotionally distressed and have taken time to consider all the above points and your options.

- Live your life. If you have explored all avenues and you decide to stay, then it will be necessary to come to terms with this decision and continue to live the best life you can.

RECONCILING PROBLEMS

If you have decided to stay in your relationship, then working through identified areas of disagreement is essential for reconciliation and moving forwards. Reconciliation takes time and commitment and can be very emotionally challenging as you work towards the outcome and the answers you need. Consider the following questions and action points.

- Appreciate that people change. All relationships have challenges, and many things can change over time, leading to one or more partners feeling differently about being in the relationship. It can help to appreciate that people don't always grow together at the same time and relationship breakdown can be a normal part of the lifecycle. Be kind and compassionate to yourself about the situation you find yourself in.

- Be real. Being open and honest is an essential part of this process. Both of you need to have an agreed understanding of why the relationship broke down in the first place, and to agree on what needs to change, for reconciliation to work and for the relationship to be different this time. This can be worked through with a therapist if necessary, so that a reasonable, unbiased plan can be drawn up for both parties to work on.

- Fully resolve the past. Work through your differences fully so that you don't keep throwing old past behaviours back in when you hit a tough time. Revenge for what has gone before needs to be off the table.

- Reconcile for the right reasons. Be sure that when you enter the reconciliation process that you're not doing so because you feel bad or guilty or that it's expected of you. If you are doing it because you genuinely want to reconcile there is a much better chance of this process working.

- Shake things up a bit. Just because you have decided you are going to try does not mean you have to go back to how things were, spend all your time together or even move back in together if you have spent time apart since separating. Go at your own pace and stagger this part of your life in a way that allows you to manage your emotions and not overwhelm yourself.

- Be on the same page. A shared vision for the future helps to keep you both on track. Create this together and agree on it. You could both agree to write your vision on a separate piece of paper, then compare notes and then come to an agreed outcome. That vision might include details such as respecting each other, listening to each other, having fun together, prioritising the relationship, reassessing the relationship each month, taking holidays together three times a year, moving back in together after six months and sharing all household duties equally.

RECONCILING AFTER A BETRAYAL

If betrayal has been part of your relationship and you are trying to reconcile with your partner, there are additional action points to consider:

- Set boundaries. The person who had the affair must remove the third party from their life immediately. That means no social media contact, their details must be deleted from their phone, no attendance at groups where the third party would be present, and a complete cut-off. They will need to let their partner know that they have done this and they are fully committed to reconciling.

- Apologise. A full and sincere apology will be needed for the person who was betrayed.

- Needing answers. If you have been betrayed, there will, no doubt, be questions you have about the betrayal. Rather than letting this absorb your thoughts 24/7, set aside a fixed period of time each week (say, 20 minutes) to talk about the betrayal. The person who had the affair will need to give true answers to questions so that both parties understand fully how and why the betrayal came about. These answers shouldn't contain any unnecessary details or images which may disturb your partner in the future. If you are the person asking questions then really consider if the answer will help your understanding and your recovery rather than fuel obsessive thoughts and triggers.

- Allow time to talk. Set aside a weekly meeting for the two of you to discuss how the reconciliation is going and if there are areas or interactions that need improving or could have been handled differently.

- Access professional help. If talking isn't working or you don't feel safe to talk, then get on touch with a therapist for couples counselling so you can both learn how to communicate better in a safe environment.

COPING WITH DIVORCE

Going through a divorce or ending a relationship, whether your choice or not, is a painful process. Understanding the factors which led to the divorce can help you to move on and raise awareness of how you interacted within the relationship and help clarify what you want and expect from a future relationship. Here are some actions you can take to help:

- Contact a therapist. Many people suffer from depression and ill health after a relationship breakdown. Thoughts like 'how could this happen to me?', 'how could my partner do this to me?', 'why didn't I see the red flags?' or 'what's wrong with me?' are common. There are many unanswered questions that many people don't get the answer to, making closure complicated. If some thoughts and feelings continually ruminate, then contact a therapist to work through them. You may want to work through your anger, shame and feelings of failure.

- Process your loss. Often a relationship breakdown can be accompanied by a period of grieving and loss. Grief is a natural reaction to loss. Time, love and energy invested in the relationship you couldn't ultimately save feels wasted. And it hurts. You might also grieve for the future you had planned that will now not materialise and the loss of the 'traditional' family unit. Processing this loss can take time. Sometimes it is better to take issues away from your friendship circle to process because then you use your friendship group for exactly what they are there for: friendship.

- Protect your identity. You may feel lost now that the role of being a partner, spouse or full-time parent is no longer part of your identity. Work on the other aspects of your life and realise you are more than just a partner: you may be a friend, a work colleague, a group member, a neighbour, a sibling or a parent.

- Prioritise self-care. Looking after yourself is essential. If you have children together, or you work with your partner, the breakdown of the relationship isn't the last time you are going to see your partner. You will need to be strong to create and uphold boundaries about how you interact together in front of colleagues or your family. Eat well and exercise. It's too easy to feel like giving up when your life has taken a different direction, but life does go on, so it helps if you are well-nourished and healthy to deal with the next stage (see the action points in both Health and Spirituality sections).

- Stay calm. Physical sensations of anxiety and anger can play havoc after a nasty separation, so try and keep the body calm as possible. Try meditation, relaxation and be around people where you can just be yourself and don't have to put on a front. This will help reduce stress and help trigger your PNS. (See the action points in Relaxation.)

- Work on your self-esteem. A relationship breakdown, especially if you are the one who has been left can trigger a period of self-doubt so begin to build yourself back up. (See action points in Self-esteem.)
- Expand your friendship group. Now that your partner has gone, you could have a lot of time on your hands. You may not be ready to date again, so expand your social circle. (See action points in Play.)
- Access support. Call on the support of family and friends if you need practical help such as developing a new routine, getting support with school runs, or financial advice now you are solely responsible for bills.
- Understand the legal process. Get legal advice to ensure you are supported through the divorce process.
- Learn from the experience. Understand that a relationship breakdown takes two people, and it can be helpful to be aware of your part. It might be your partner who decided to leave or who had an affair but take some time to reflect in hindsight on what you might have said or done differently. You can then take this knowledge and support yourself, using it in a future relationship should you wish to date again.

BEING SINGLE

Being single in midlife can be due to a variety of reasons: loss of a spouse or partner, the availability of alternative lifestyles, and changing societal views on the importance of marriage or a relationship breakdown.

Part 3: Recalibrating the New You

For some people, being single will be a welcome relief, whereas others may struggle because it is the first time in many years that they haven't been part of a couple.

The issues that may arise with being single are, typically, feeling lonely, lacking emotional support, recovering from relationship breakdown, looking after children, and wanting intimacy and sex.

The population of never-married men and women is expanding. Being single does not necessarily mean feeling alone. I was single for eight years in my 40s and enjoyed this time not being with a partner. Single people have fulfilling lives through their friends, family and community, just like everyone else. If you want to be single or remain single and thrive, here are some action points you could consider:

- Find and build your community. Research shows midlifers spend more time with family and friends. This won't apply to all midlifers, of course, as it'll depend on their upbringing, cultural background, individual relationships, personal values and personalities. Some people will be single by choice, some people will become single due to circumstances, such as divorce or the death of a partner or spouse. By expanding your community, you lessen the risk of becoming lonely.

- Maximise fun. Take the opportunity to decide how you want to spend any free time you have. Explore your genuine interests. (See action points in Play.)

- Embrace solitude. Being alone isn't for everyone as many people experience it as loneliness and not a positive experience. For others being alone and not having any demands on them can be rejuvenating and a chance to consider their situation and think deeply about their life. It is a time to consider if they feel they are heading in the right direction and making good choices for themselves.

  Getting the balance right between spending time with others and spending time alone is really important. Keeping a social network that you can return to after your period of solitude can create a good balance in your life. You don't necessarily have to go away to experience solitude; you can find it in your own home in a room where you won't be disturbed, or go for a walk and sit on a park bench quietly. You could be engaged in an activity on your own such as reading or practising yoga. The most important thing is that if you know solitude is a great way for you to revitalise yourself, then commit to doing this for yourself, putting a time and place in your diary and letting others know not to disturb you.

- Find contentment in being single. More people choose to be single after having spent years in a relationship or having the responsibility of bringing up children. Some will see this as a temporary situation and have every intention of finding a partner in the future after some time being single. Work at creating a contented meaningful life on your own because the more contented you are being single the more able you are to be objective about possible future partners and whether they would enhance and help fulfil your life or not.

- Enjoy the freedom. Being single has many benefits such as being able to make your own decisions without the need to consult a partner. You have time to focus on what you genuinely enjoy and the freedom to do it when you want to, without having to negotiate with a partner.

- Challenge assumptions. Many people assume you have a lot of time on your hands when you're single but that isn't necessarily the case. You may be busy with work, parenting, friendships, hobbies, and chores. Don't be afraid to make people aware that you have a full life and are not always 'on call'.

- Strengthen support. Maximise your non-romantic friendships and ensure you have social networks and friends to support you. Social support is very meaningful when you are single. (See action points in Social.)

- Reassess life. If you are single and the quality of your life isn't good enough, but this is unrelated to your being single, then clarify what it is in your life that you are unhappy with. It might be finances, lack of intimacy with another, or work-related. See which areas of your life scored low for dissatisfaction in your life by going back to Exercise 1: The personal balance wheel (page 18) and considering the 14 areas of your life to see which ones score low for dissatisfaction. Seeing where the values you identified are poorly reflected in an area could help account for your overall unhappiness.
- Know yourself better. If being single is a temporary situation for you and you want to return being in a relationship at some point, it can be helpful to do some self-exploration and clarify your expectations. Be clear about your boundaries, be prepared to enforce them, and be clear about what you want/don't want and will/won't accept in a new relationship.
- Don't put up with 'single shaming'. This can happen because of other people's negative biases about people who don't have a partner. You can make it clear that you have a full life and are not sad and lonely and not waiting for the next partner to come along – this is your lifestyle choice.

MIDLIFE DATING

You may have reached midlife as a single person or become suddenly single in midlife following a relationship breakdown, divorce or by becoming widowed. You may be facing a whole new world of midlife dating. Knowing what you want is key here to a successful dating life. Starting to date again after a long period can be a little intimidating but also great fun. Here are some actions to think about:

- Understand yourself. Make sure you are emotionally ready for dating. Are you still working through the grief accompanying the death of a partner or the anger of betrayal. Processing emotions related to your past can result in being more emotionally available to people in the future.

- Know what you need. It helps to be clear about what you are looking for now in midlife. Are you looking for friendship or a committed serious relationship? There is no need to repeat the first half of life again and find someone, settle down, move into together and get married. You can have a relationship, live separately and see each other at weekends, it's all up for negotiation.

- Be ready to make the time. When you begin a new relationship it can take time, effort and energy to get to know someone, listen to them, tell your story, and dress yourself up so you feel good. Are you ready to invest? Do you actually want to date, or do you just need more socials out with your friends?

- Don't feel pressurised by friends to date. People who haven't experienced the heartbreak and disappointment of the breakup of a serious relationship might find it hard to appreciate just how daunting this stage can be. Sit them down and have an honest and frank talk with them, letting them know that you feel pressured by them and that it doesn't help. Give them ideas of other ways they can support you.

- Set your intimacy boundaries. If you just want coffee, friendship and no sex then say so. That way you are clear from the start with the people you meet.

- Take time out. If you have been in an abusive relationship in the past, take time out and invest in sessions with a professional to understand and stop this cycle of abuse. This may include working through past trauma, creating new boundaries in your life and clarifying what you will and will not tolerate in a relationship.

- Respect yourself. If you are a people pleaser and tend to deprioritise your needs, then work this through with a therapist so you can knowingly not lose yourself in your next relationship.
- Work on your self-esteem. Feeling good about yourself and strong on the inside can put you in a really good position to start dating online or in person. (See action points in Self-esteem)
- Understand your relationship history. People in midlife carry with them their history of relationships. How they interact, their attachments and expectations from life and their partner, and societal and cultural expectations, shape who they are. Understanding what you are carrying is important and helpful for future healthy relationships.
- See a therapist. Understanding why previous relationships haven't been fulfilling for you creates an opportunity for you to change your life course within a new relationship. This analysis can take time to ensure that you don't just go straight back in and repeat your romantic patterns – whether that be marrying another narcissist or neglecting your own needs.
- Get to know yourself. Before you begin dating it can really help to be comfortable with being on your own because this can help you to choose an appropriate partner rather than entering a relationship because you feel that you need one. Get to know yourself better with the help of a therapist, strengthen your friendships, try new things to see what you truly enjoy, maximise your self-care, get rid of anything that makes you feel lonely (such as photos of your ex-partner), and unfollow social media accounts that make you feel inadequate.
- Be authentic on dates. It's really hard to keep up a front and hide your true feelings or any hurt you might be experiencing. If dating is too much, then tick the 'just friends' box to start

with on your profile. Make your profile honest and start as you mean to go on.

- Choose wisely. You don't have to make an immediate decision. Take time to get to know someone and see if they have the same values, morals and lifestyle choices as you.
- Know what you're looking for. Carefully consider the qualities you are looking for in a partner and make sure they are up-to-date and don't just reflect your set of requirements from a younger age.
- Don't keep it a secret. Be prepared to tell family and friends you trust you are dating so you can access their support if you need it.
- Take your time with intimacy. It can take time to feel relaxed and comfortable with someone after you have had the same partner for many years. Wait for someone who understands that you want to take it slow, or is happy to take it at your pace, and someone you feel comfortable with and feel the connection is right. Equally, it is okay to know you are an adult who may enjoy exploring intimacy in more casual experiences or at a faster pace in an early relationship. As long as you are feeling safe, in control and happy with your choices (and not pressured into making choices you aren't comfortable with or that don't feel safe) then you can be empowered to explore this area however you want without judgement. (See action points in Sex and intimacy.)
- Keep an open mind to new experiences, so long as you feel safe enough. If you feel a little scared, work out if this is anxiety or excitement before you say no.
- Don't rely on apps alone. Get out there in the real world. (See action points in Play and Social.)

SEX AND INTIMACY

Physical and mental challenges can affect sex and intimacy in midlife. Declining hormone levels mean age-related changes such as erectile dysfunction, bodily changes, painful penetration, issues around altering body image, vaginal dryness and low libido can create issues within relationships of differing needs, reduced physical intimacy and lack of physical affection. Sex and intimacy problems are often intertwined with relationship issues, often related to differing needs, emotional distancing, poor communication and betrayal. (See action points in Relationships.)

In this section, I will tackle sex and intimacy issues which can arise both within a couple and as a single person.

SEX AND INTIMACY AS A COUPLE

If you are in a committed relationship then sex can be a really important source of fun, pleasure, intimacy and connectedness. It provides a valuable outlet for physical touch, energy, and vitality, and it also can help reduce stress and improve sleep.

For many people, sex will be an important part of their identity and when libido reduces in middle age it can affect their identity and be a main trigger for a midlife crisis.

If you are in a relationship, it is not so much the amount of sex you are having, but that both parties are satisfied with the amount and quality of the sex. It is possible to have intimacy in a relationship without sexual contact, but it helps if this has been discussed openly within the relationship and agreed upon and both partners are content with the agreement.

Without a doubt, communication keeps relationships together. Being able to talk openly and honestly with your partner about any concerns or desires that you have increases the chance of you both feeling connected to one another and being more satisfied in the relationship. It means needs and desires have been expressed and, hopefully, acted upon or negotiated satisfactorily. Here are some action points:

- Consider professional guidance. If communication is a struggle, then engage with a psychosexual therapist who can teach you how to communicate in a safe, non-judgemental environment. This can help with issues within relationships such as low libido, and difficulty having sex due to hormonal changes in perimenopause, menopause or erectile dysfunction. Communication can help people to understand the mental and physical issues going on for their partners, so that they can be more compassionate and understanding, whether sexual problems are of a temporary nature or something that needs to be permanently integrated into their sex life.

- Tackle poor body image. A poor body image can increase sexual anxiety and lower sexual esteem, particularly for women. To improve the way you feel about your body, look after yourself physically with what you eat and drink and maintain a healthy diet and weight. A poor body image can start in our mind, so work on your self-esteem and mental health. (See action points in Self-esteem and Health.)

- Experiment with new sexual positions. Staying open to exploration and trying something new can add excitement and variety to your sexual encounters.

- Prioritise your sex life. Setting time aside with a partner to develop and nurture this part of your relationship is important.
- Work on the relationship as a whole. Keep the relationship caring, trustful and respectful outside of sex. A good relationship can add to a better sexual connection.
- Take responsibility. Get to understand each other's preferences and be responsible for your own pleasure. Knowing what works for you and becoming informed about the body and stimulation points can be useful. Seeing a sex therapist can help the two of you communicate better about your needs.
- Experiment with different types of intimacy. There are several kinds of intimacy, which can all take place outside of the bedroom; emotional intimacy, sexual intimacy, physical intimacy and intellectual intimacy.
    - ↠ Emotional intimacy is being transparent with your partner about your feelings. Tell them how you feel about them. It is not always easy to share these thoughts with them. You can feel vulnerable and exposed as you share these aspects of your life with someone else. Overcome vulnerability by setting boundaries before these types of discussions are had so that you feel safer disclosing this personal information. Make sure that they are someone who will appreciate the effort you are making in being more available emotionally and that they are prepared to do the same. Before sharing thoughts, write down what you know about yourself and what you want, to get these ideas clear in your head and improve your confidence in voicing them.
    - ↠ Intellectual intimacy is about sharing ideas about life, the universe and just about everything and anything else. Chatting and sharing ideas and stories and being open to each other's varying points of view and having stimulat-

ing conversations and taking time to be curious about one another can bring a couple closer together.

→ Spiritual intimacy can be about sharing each other's beliefs and spiritual practices which can bring you closer together. Having meaningful conversations and talking about your relationship and your hope for the relationship can help nourish it and enhance your sense of purpose and meaning in the world.

→ Physical intimacy doesn't always have to be about sex. It can mean holding, looking into each other's eyes, caressing your partner all over their body or just cuddling. The main thing is intimate physical contact.

- Connect with each other. Soul gazing is becoming a popular way of connecting. Here you sit opposite each other, gazing into each other's eyes, with your knees touching, for three to five minutes. You can talk during this time or listen to music. It can be a useful way to reconnect if sex has been absent from your relationship for a while.

- Use porn to get you going. Different people have different opinions on porn for many reasons. But if this is something that works for you and your partner and helps spice up your sex life, then don't be afraid to explore this.

- Swing. Many couples these days choose an alternative lifestyle, such as swinging, to revitalise their sex life. This can work well if both parties are agreeable to their partner having sex with another person.

- Understand your body. Get to know exactly what turns you on and ask for it. Sexual needs and stimulation change as you age, and as your partner isn't a mind reader, you'll need to explain what you want them to do.

- Keep all your sexual organs in good working order. Anyone who has had a baby will have been encouraged by midwives to see pelvic floor exercises to strengthen their internal muscles. Regular small bouts of exercise can make a difference in how you feel and add to your enjoyment of sex.
- Change the venue. Why not vary the places where you have sex, you can try in your car, or your garden, it doesn't always have to be in the bedroom.
- Expand your sexual repertoire. Buy a sex book and choose a new position to try out every time you have sex.

SEX AND INTIMACY AS A SINGLE PERSON

With an increasing number of single midlifers, an absence of sex and intimacy can also become problematic. You can increase the amount of sex you have if you are not in a committed relationship by implementing these actions:

- Date. Going on more dates to increase your chance of having sex with someone. If you expand your social life and join groups, this will put you in the company of more people and you may meet someone you'd like to have sex with there. (See action points in Play and Social.)
- Buy sex toys. Masturbation allows you to attend to your own needs without involving anyone else. It can help reduce stress, help sleep, strengthen pelvic floor muscles, and improve overall well-being because of the endorphins the brain releases on climax.
- Let go of societal expectations. You don't have to save yourself for the third date if there is passion and desire for each other on the first date. Enjoy safe sex. You are allowed to do whatever you want with your own body.

- Schedule sex. If you've got a diary and some free time then why not use it productively and schedule in sex with a friend you have agreed to have a sexual relationship with, with no ties.
- Increase casual hook-ups. This can lead to fun experiences without commitment. Apps like Tinder and Hinge are good for this.
- Swing. A swingers lifestyle for single people can work well and sexual needs can be met without the need for commitment or a relationship.
- Pace yourself. However you decide to increase your sexual activity, ensure you do it at a pace that is right for you.

JOY

Joy is a feeling of great pleasure, happiness or delight and for many is an area of life which needs improvement and attention. Joy isn't necessarily a constant feeling we experience but it can feel wonderful if your general experience of life is that it contains moments of joy. In midlife joy can be hard to find in amongst work and ageing parent responsibilities, raising children and health issues.

Joy can be experienced as passing brief emotions while you are engaged in an activity such as eating a wonderfully delicious treat or over a longer period of time such as when you are connecting with nature. Joy can be found by engaging in activities which fill your life in a meaningful way or through spending time with people you love being around.

If you strive to cultivate joy in your life, you can experience an overall sense of well-being, fulfilment and contentment, as you know you are engaging in activities or friendships which bring you pleasure.

A key element of joy to be aware of is that you can practise finding moments of joy even when life is challenging. People can find moments of joy when they are grieving or struggling with extreme stress or unhappiness. You do not have to wait for life to be perfect, happy, or wonderful, to be able to find joy.

To increase the amount of joy in your life, try some of the following action points:

- Practise gratitude. Take time out daily, or at the end of meditation practice, to reflect on the things that you have in your life that you're grateful for. This might be friends; a pet; a warm, safe, cosy bed; a loving partner or peace of mind. This focus on the positive aspects of your life can increase joy and contentment and help you experience more positive emotions in your life, making you more able to feel grateful and giving you more capacity for kindness and compassion for yourself and others. (See action points in Spirituality.)

- Notice joy in the small moments. Teach yourself to notice wonderful simple pleasures such as a rainbow on a rainy day, a baby's smile, the smell of baking bread, your favourite table being free at your favourite coffee shop, or an unexpected lie-in.

- Spend time with people who love you. People who support you unconditionally can be an immense pleasure. Loving human connection can be a source of support and fulfilment in life and can increase emotional support and reduce loneliness. Studies have shown that this type of connection also improves physical health and a sense of well-being. Social connections have been linked to lower rates of various health problems, such as heart disease and stroke and shown to strengthen our immune systems. The connections that produce the most joy are authentic, empathic and full of trust, support, good communication, shared interests and a shared sense of humanity as there is nothing like a good laugh to increase the joy in your life. (See action points in Social.)

- Stay well within yourself. Find time to relax and reduce stress so you feel your life is balanced. Yoga and relaxation and meditation can help calm your body after a stressful day and increase the feeling of well-being. Eat a healthy diet and prioritise good sleep. (See action points in Health.)

- Choose your work wisely. Find a job that is meaningful to you and based on your values. It can be invaluable to take time to consider what aspects of your current work matter to you, and to others or society, and see if this is sufficient for your needs. Many people experience joy when their work contributes to a greater cause. When you find work which aligns with your values, you can experience a sense of fulfilment and reward. (See action points in Work.)

- Set goals. Achieving goals and then celebrating them can be a great source of contentment and joy in your home and working life. Set goals which are achievable over time, large or small, which you can then feel proud of achieving.

Whatever it is that works for you and brings even a small sense of joy and delight, make time to do more of it and prioritise this.

SELF-ESTEEM

Self-esteem develops in childhood. It is influenced by our environment and by our personal relationships and how we are treated by others, such as family friends, and other influential people, including such as teachers, and the messages we receive about ourselves from them. Our self-esteem is also impacted by our successes and failures and can continue to evolve throughout our lives. It is centred around our sense of worth and how we value and perceive ourselves. Healthy self-esteem can lead to a sense of wellness, and it can support us psychologically and emotionally even when things are going wrong.

In midlife often self-esteem can take a bit of a battering because recognising and appreciating all our good qualities can be challenging alongside not knowing who we are, bodily changes, feeling like our life doesn't fit, that we're on the wrong path, or that we should have achieved more by now.

Self-esteem can change over time but for it to last and be meaningful it takes time. It is not an overnight process for a truly long-lasting sense of self-worth and positive self-esteem.

Here are some actions to enhance your own self-esteem:

- Keep a watchful eye on yourself. Be active in creating self-esteem as it is not fixed and can change over time: it is not something that can be improved or decreased overnight. Building and improving self-esteem is a process that involves making positive changes in one's life and developing a more positive self-image. This process can involve seeking out supportive relationships, setting and achieving personal goals, and engaging in activities that bring a sense of accomplishment and fulfilment.

- Spread the risk. Allow your self-esteem to be based on different aspects of yourself and your personality so you are never reliant on needing one particular area of your life to go well so that you feel good. This applies especially if you have relied on your looks to support your self-esteem throughout your life, because as you get older, your looks may begin to change. If you don't feel as attractive as you once did, this can impact self-esteem. If your self-esteem is spread over different aspects of your life such as your work, how you support others, how well your body functions, how kind you are or how your life is aligned with your values, then you have a greater chance of keeping it high.

- Maximise self-compassion. If you practise self-compassion, you can nurture yourself at difficult times in your life to help you continue to feel good about yourself, even though things may not be going well outwardly.

- Watch your inner dialogue. Keep your self-talk positive and minimise self-criticism. If your self-talk is compassionate, understanding and encouraging then you can boost your self-esteem and reduce reliance on others for an external boost and rely on the self for encouragement and support.

- Set goals. Make sure they are achievable and meaningful and work towards them as this will increase your sense of accomplishment and achievement.

- Maximise self-care. Eat healthily and concentrate on a refreshing sleep regime. Exercise regularly to boost natural endorphins and feel good about your body. In a body-obsessed world, it can be very easy to be down on yourself because of how you look but high self-esteem can counter these societal expectations. (See action points in Health.)

- Find your people. Fill your life with supportive people who love you for yourself and are engaged with any changes you want to make and encourage you.
- See a therapist. If you increase your ability to self-reflect you will create a deeper understanding of the person you are and what is important to you. This can then inform future actions and decisions and create a sense of being true to yourself, which in turn can boost self-esteem. Learning from the wrong turns you might have taken in the past with an understanding of why you took them can boost self-awareness, creating a more informed way for you to love yourself.
- Try something new. Do something which takes you outside of your comfort zone, so you can feel good about yourself for growing as a person.

Self-esteem is never set and needs constant care and attention so that it remains high. If you can boost this yourself, it puts you in a very strong position for continued well-being.

COMFORT IN LIFE

What constitutes comfort in life will differ from person to person. For some, it will not be about having material goods or being able to buy anything they want, but will be about being free to choose, having a safe secure environment, or doing the job that they want to do.

Comfort in life is very subjective and can mean different things to different people but, generally, it refers to a state of well-being and general contentment about how you exist in the world in a way that allows you to feel comfortable within yourself, relaxed, secure and at ease.

There are various factors which can contribute to this relaxed state. Good relationships, for example, or feeling you are achieving your goals or living your best life, enjoying how you spend your time whether at work or socially, looking after your physical health, and contentment related to your living standards and situation. Comfort in life doesn't have to be money-related or based on the feeling of financial security, although this can make a difference for some people.

Comfort in life can be impacted in midlife as people juggle additional responsibilities, busy schedules, health challenges, changing family dynamics and career changes.

To improve your comfort, consider the following actions:

- Stay well. Take care of your physical health if you are aware that this has been lacking in the past. Prioritise sleeping, healthy eating habits and exercise. To be comfortable with how your body functions and to feel that you are giving yourself your best shot at health can be very reassuring. (See action points in Health.)

- Be active. Make sure activities are centred around what you truly enjoy and not carried out for the good of someone else or because it is what you think you should be doing. Good fun activities require very little effort, and you shouldn't have to force yourself to participate in them.

- Let the body be your guide. Finding and experiencing comfort in life is an ongoing challenge. Tune into your body's reaction to anything that you change and notice if it no longer feels as satisfying as it once did and consider why this is and what needs to change.

- Be with the right people. Being around people who are authentic and genuinely want the best for you can provide a stable secure base in life where you can feel cared for. This gives you a great platform on which to tackle the world, or even to stretch yourself a little further in an area of your life where you feel a bit of backup would go a long way to helping you achieve what you want.

- Relax. Make sure you practise relaxation techniques and give your body a chance to relax by triggering your PNS. Meditation, yoga, or relaxation exercises can help you to do this and so throughout the day you can practise getting your body and breathing into a less stressful position. You can also explore other ways to engage in self-care or restful, soothing or restorative activities to activate the PNS e.g. massage, taking a bath, sitting in nature, listening to music. (See action points in Relaxation.)

- Ensure your home is happy. If you have a home that you enjoy being in and you can afford to live there, this can give you a great sense of well-being. If it also has all the essentials you need and your home doesn't feel overcluttered to you, then a living space can feel comfortable and inviting.

RELAXATION

Relaxing both your mind and your body can improve the quality of your life and sense of overall well-being. Making time to do this is important, as busy lifestyles mean often if this isn't planned then days might pass before you have prioritised this aspect of your life.

It might be as simple as allowing yourself a proper lunch hour, or getting up early before work or before anyone else gets up to engage in activity to slow down your body and relax your mind. These skills are also helpful for waking in the night if you are restless and can't get back to sleep and can be used as a precursor to sleep. Get advice from your doctor if you are in any doubt about the form of relaxation that would suit you, given any medical conditions you might have. Here are some action points to guide you:

- Let your body relax. You can use the three techniques to help trigger your **PNS** in Chapter 7 (page 89) to help you to relax, and see the meditation action points in Spirituality.

- Experiment with yoga or tai chi. Both these disciplines can offer a plethora of health and wellness. Not only do they improve balance, strength and flexibility and reduce pain, but they can also raise your mood and enhance thinking skills. Yoga involves holding poses, while tai chi is performed with constant movements, like a dance in a slow continuous movement.

- Try green exercise. Spending time outdoors can create feelings of joy and wonderment. Research clearly shows the beneficial effects of nature on physical, psychological, social and emotional well-being. So, join a walking or rambling group, go horse riding, kite flying, cycling, or gardening.

- Access a CBT Therapist. CBT can help calm and quieten down a chattering mind to help with relaxation. Reduce negative anxious thoughts by following the information in Chapter 7 (page 92).

- Distract yourself. The brain cannot actively think about two things at the same time. So, keep your brain focused by engaging in an activity which you can get absorbed into and enjoy.

- Try re-energizing activities. Soothing and restful activities such as facials, listening to music, going to a spa, having a bath, baking, reading, and having a lie in, can all help the body to relax.

- Choose people wisely. Mix with the people who lift you and make you feel safe and secure. (See action points in Social.)

- Have fun. Do things that enable you to have fun. (See action points in Play.)

- Reduce work stress. If work is a barrier to relaxation, then look at enhancing your life outside work. (See action points in Work.)

AND SO WE COME TO THE END OF THE JOURNEY. I HOPE I HAVE provided you with all the understanding and motivation you need to live a fulfilling midlife and beyond.

Join me on Facebook at The Midlife Crisis Handbook Support Group if you need extra support from likeminded midlifers and on my website (www.drjuliehannan.com) for specific advice, resources and blogs about varying aspects of midlife.

I look forward to seeing you there and wish you well.

Julie x

GLOSSARY

Term	Definition
andropause	A condition in midlife men when they experience a loss of interest in life and mood irritability. Often attributed to reduced testosterone levels but more likely to be related to lifestyle factors or psychological difficulties.
archetype	An archetype can be a pattern of behaviour, a character or a typical example of a person or thing.
autonomic nervous system (ANS)	A network of nerves which regulate certain body processes, such as blood pressure and breathing. Consists of the SNS and PNS.
cognitive behavioural therapy (CBT)	A talking therapy that focuses on thoughts, beliefs and attitudes to help you solve problems.
communitas	A word to describe the special bond between people who are experiencing liminality.
cortisol	A steroid hormone and helps regulate the body's response to stress.
Dante	Dante Alighieri was an Italian poet, writer and philosopher, 1265–1321.
dopamine	A brain chemical that influences mood. Known as the 'feel-good' hormone.

epinephrine	A hormone produced by the adrenal glands produce to help regulate organ functions.
endorphins	Chemicals produced in the body to reduce pain and increase pleasure.
existentialism	Existentialism is a philosophy that explores human existence and our lived experiences. Existentialists believe in the uniqueness of the individual and that each of us is responsible for making choices and creating purpose and meaning in our own lives.
external locus of control	Carries the belief that other things or people determine what happens to you.
fight/flight/freeze response	An automatic physiological response to a perceived dangerous event.
Freud	Sigmund Freud (1856–1939) was an Austrian neurologist and the founding father of psychoanalysis.
gestalt therapy	A form of psychotherapy which concentrates on the individual's experience in the present moment.
givens	Those things in life which cannot be changed.
Goethe	Johann Wolfgang von *Goethe* (1749–1832) was a German poet and playwright.
homeostasis	Refers to a person's ability to regulate various physiological processes within their body and keep internal states stable and balanced.
hormone replacement therapy (HRT)	A treatment used to relieve the symptoms of menopause.

Glossary

individuation	Refers to the process of forming a stable personality. Jung saw it as the focus for the individual for the second half of life.
internal locus of control	Carries the belief that you are in control of what happens to you.
Jean-Paul Sartre	An existentialist and French playwright (1905-1980).
liminality or liminal space	A liminal space or liminality is a metaphorical place where you are in between identities.
menopause	A point in time 12 months after a woman's last menstrual cycle.
norepinephrine	A naturally occurring hormone in the body produced to mobilise the brain and body for action.
oxytocin	A naturally occurring hormone in the body positively impacting relaxation.
parasympathetic nervous system (PNS)	A network of nerves which can be activated to relax the body after periods of stress or danger. It regulates rest and digest functions.
person-environment fit (P-E fit) theory	The degree to which people and environmental characteristics fit.
psyche	Jung believed the psyche to be a self-regulating system similar to the body that aims to find balance between opposing qualities while striving for personal growth.
psychopathology	The study of abnormal mental states.
seasonal affective disorder (SAD)	A type of depression related to changes in seasons.
somatic	Relating to the body.

sympathetic nervous system (SNS)	The sympathetic nervous system controls our fight or flight response by speeding up heart rate and pushing blood to areas of the body needing increased oxygen.
testosterone	A hormone found in humans that testicles or ovaries produce.
Virgil	An ancient Roman poet of the Augustan period, 70–19 BC.
visceral	A physical reaction to a non-physical experience.

REFERENCES

1. Jaques, E. (1965). Death and the Midlife Crisis. *International Journal of Psychoanalysis*.

2. Lachman, M.E. (2001). *Handbook of midlife development*. New York: Wiley.

3. Worldometer (2020). *Life Expectancy by Country and in the World (2020)*. [online] Worldometers.info. Available at: https://www.worldometers.info/demographics/life-expectancy/.

4. Jung, C. G. (1963). *Memories, dreams, reflections*. Crown Publishing Group/Random House.

5. Covey, S. R. (1989). *The 7 habits of highly effective people: restoring the character ethic*. New York: Simon and Schuster.

6. Frankl, V.E. (1962). *Man's Search for Meaning: an introduction to logotherapy*. Boston: Beacon Press.

7. Ware, B. (2012). *The top five regrets of the dying: a life transformed by the dearly departing*. Carlsbad, California: Hay House.

8. Maslow, A.H. (1954). *Motivation and Personality*. New York: Harper & Row.

9. French, J.R., Caplan, R.D., and Van Harrison, R. (1982). *The mechanisms of job stress and strain* (Vol. 7). Chichester: Wiley.

10. Harrison, R. V. (1978). Person–environment fit and job stress. In Cooper, C.L. and Payne, R. (eds.), *Stress at work*. New York: Wiley, pp. 175–205.

11. Harrison, R. V. (1985). The person-environment fit model and the study of job stress. In Beehr, T.A. and Bhagat, R.S (eds.), *Human stress and cognition in organizations*. New York: Wiley pp. 23–55.

12. Freud, S. (1922). *Introductory Lectures on Psycho-Analysis*.

13. Jung, C.G. (2015). 'Paracelsus' in *The spirit in man, art and literature*. London: Routledge.

14. Ali, M. *Muhammad Ali Quotes, www.goodreads.com.* [Online.] Available at: https://www.goodreads.com/quotes/41404-the-man-who-views-the-world-at-50-the-same. [Accessed 10 February 2023].

15. Jung, C.G. (1931). *Visions Seminar.*

16. Alighieri, D., (eds. Cary, H.F., and Doré, G.) (1935). *The Divine Comedy of Dante Alighieri: Inferno, Purgatory, Paradise.* New York: The Union Library Association.

17. Keefer, L. A., Landau, M. J., Rothschild, Z. K., and Sullivan, D. (2012). Attachment to objects as compensation for close others' perceived unreliability. *Journal of Experimental Social Psychology, 48*(4), pp. 912–917.

18. Beck, J. S. (2011). Cognitive behavior therapy: basics and beyond (2nd ed.). Guilford Press.

19. Barnard, L.K., and Curry, J.F. (2011). Self-Compassion: Conceptualizations, Correlates, and Interventions. *Review of General Psychology*, 15, pp. 289–303.

20. MacBeth, A., and Gumley, A. (2012). Exploring compassion: a metaanalysis of the association between self-compassion and psychopathology. Clinical Psychology Review, 32(6). pp. 545–552.

21. Neff, K. D. (2003). Self-Compassion: An Alternative Conceptualization of a Healthy Attitude Toward Oneself. *Self and Identity*, 2(2), pp. 85–101.

22. Barnard, L.K., and Curry, J.F. (2011). Self-Compassion: Conceptualizations, Correlates, and Interventions. *Review of General Psychology*, 15, pp. 289–303.

23. Turner, V. (1969). The Ritual Process: Structure and Anti-structure. Chicago: Aldine Publishing.

24. Stein, M. (1984). *In midlife.* Dallas: Spring Publications.

25. Czarniawska, B., & Mazza, C. (2003). Consulting as a Liminal Space. *Human Relations*, 56(3), 267–290. https://doi.org/10.1177/0018726703056003612

26. Turner, V. (1969). The Ritual Process: Structure and Anti-structure. Chicago: Aldine Publishing.

27. Aaker, J. L., Rudd, M., and Mogilner, C. (2011). If money does not make you happy, consider time, *Journal of Consumer Psychology*, 21(2), pp. 126–130.

28. Ibid.

29. Kahneman, D., Krueger, A. B., Schkade, D. A., Schwarz, N. and Stone, A. A. (2004). A survey method for characterizing daily life experience: The day reconstruction method. *Science*, 306, pp. 1776–1780.

References

30. Deschene, L. (2016). *Practice the Pause.* [online] Tiny Buddha. Available at: https://tinybuddha.com/fun-and-inspiring/practice-the-pause/ [Accessed 31 January 2023].

31. Perls, F. (1969). *Ego, Hunger, and Aggression.* New York: Random House.

32. Clarkson, P., and Cavicchia, S. (2014). Gestalt Counselling in Action (4th ed). London: Sage, p. 181.

33. Sharma, R. *Robin Sharma: Official website of the #1 bestselling author, Robin Sharma.* [Online.] Available at: https://www.robinsharma.com/ [Accessed: February 4, 2023.]

34. Williamson, M. Available at: https://www.marianne.com. [Accessed 10 February 2023].

35. BrainyQuote. (n.d.). *Jane Fonda Quotes.* [online] Available at: https://www.brainyquote.com/quotes/jane_fonda_384879. [Accessed 10 February 2023].

36. BrainyQuote. (n.d.). George Bernard Shaw Quotes. [online] Available at: https://www.brainyquote.com/quotes/george_bernard_shaw_120971 [Accessed 10 February 2023].

37. Brown, S.L., and Vaughan, C.C. (2009). *Play: how it shapes the brain, opens the imagination, and invigorates the soul.* New York, Avery.

38. Fingerman, K., and Suitor, J. (2017). Millennials and Their Parents: Implications of the New Young Adulthood for Midlife Adults. *Innovation in Aging.* 1. 10.1093/geroni/igx026.

39. Meyer, M.H.T., and Abdul-Malak, Y., (2016). Grandparenting in the United States, *Legal Issues in Global Contexts: Perspectives on Technical Communication in an International Age.* Milton Park: Taylor and Francis, pp. 1–16.

40. Bordone, V., and Arpino, B. (2016). Do Grandchildren Influence How Old You Feel? *Journal of Aging and Health*, 28(6), 1055–1072. https://doi.org/10.1177/0898264315618920

41. Brody, D.J., Pratt, L.A., and Hughes, J. (2018). Prevalence of depression among adults aged 20 and over: United States, 2013–2016. *NCHS Data Brief*, pp. 1–8.

42. Gondek, D., Bann, D., Brown, M., et al. (2021). Prevalence and early-life determinants of mid-life multimorbidity: evidence from the 1970 British birth cohort. *BMC Public Health* 21, p. 1319.

43. Chen Y., and Sloan F.A., (2015). Explaining disability trends in the U.S. elderly and near-elderly population. *Health Services Research*, 50, pp. 1528–1549.

44. Crimmins, E.M., Shim, H., Zhang, Y.S., and Kim, J.K. (2019). Differences between Men and Women in Mortality and the Health Dimensions of the Morbidity Process. *Clinical Chemistry*, 65(1): pp. 135–145.

45. Xu W.L., Atti A.R., Gatz M., Pedersen N.L., Johansson B., Fratiglioni L. Midlife overweight and obesity increase late-life dementia risk: a population-based twin study. *Neurology*, 3 May 2011, 76(18), pp. 1568–1574.

46. Chadid, S., Singer, M.R., Kreger, B.E., et al. (2018). Midlife weight gain is a risk factor for obesity-related cancer. *British Journal of Cancer* 118, pp. 1665–1671.

47. Giuntella, O., Hyde, K., Saccardo, S., and Sadoff, S. (2021). Lifestyle and mental health disruptions during COVID-19. *Proceedings of the National Academy of Sciences of the United States of America*, 118(9).

48. Hollis, J. (1998). *The Eden Project: In search of the magical other.* Toronto: Inner City Books.

Printed in Poland
by Amazon Fulfillment
Poland Sp. z o.o., Wrocław

34901082R00134